My tale.

If it's pretty, if it's ugly, only you know. But I swear I didn't tell a lie and that these affairs happened in this our land of Luanda.

(José Luandino Vieira: *Luuanda*, 1963)

A family of the musseque

Survival and development in postwar Angola

Alexia Gamito
João Francisco da Silva
Pascoal Estevão
Jack Ramiro
Vicente Albino Paulo
Victor Vunge
Bob van der Winden (ed.)

ONE WORLD ACTION

INCORPORATING THE NICARAGUA HEALTH FUND

- PUBLISHED IN ASSOCIATION WITH WORLDVIEW PUBLISHING -

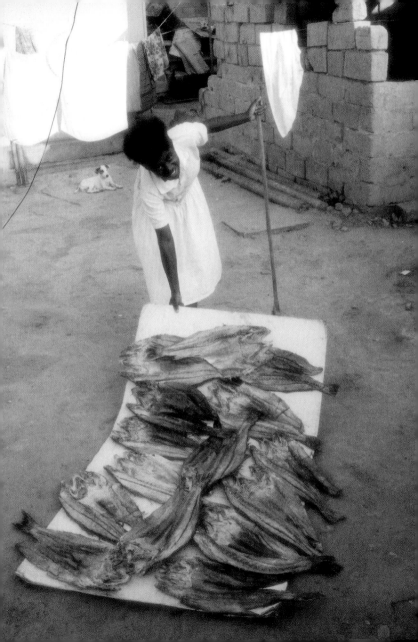

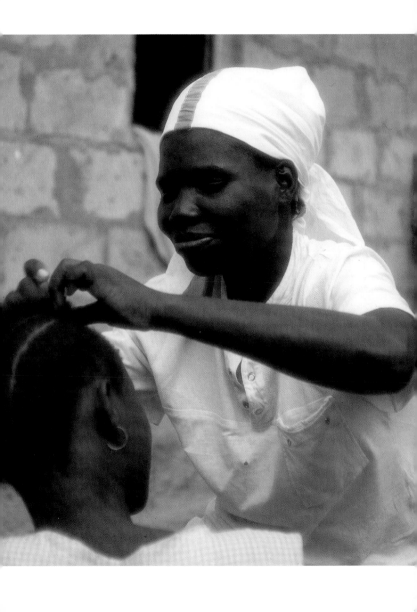

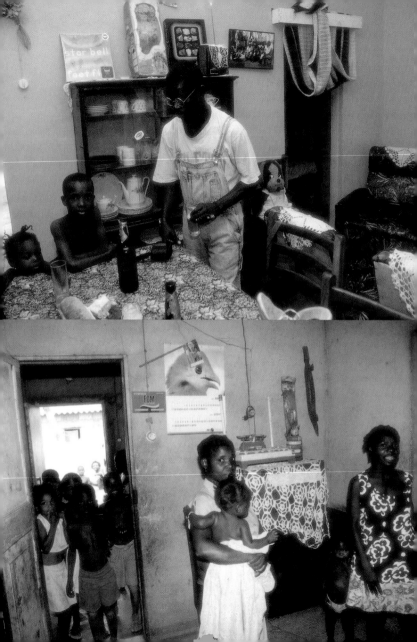

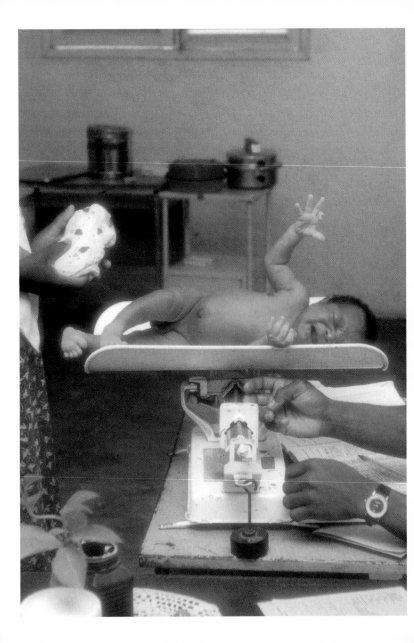

A *family of the musseque*

Survival and development in postwar Angola

We dedicate this book to the Ricardo family and all the other courageous Angolans struggling for survival and development.
For their protection, we have changed the names of the people featured in this book.

Acknowledgements

We would like to thank all the people who so kindly answered our many questions, especially the Ricardo family. Thanks to the people who took such good care of our transport: Kota Victor Manuel Samuel and Euclides Borges Simedo, who unfortunately has since died in a car accident.

Also thanks to the staff of Development Workshop and One World Action who helped us: Carlos, Lando, Romero, Nelito, Venâncio, Joaquin, Viegas, Rufino, Furtado, Adão, Puna, Hernani, Sadi, Sandra, Teresa, Joana, Graciano, Orquidea, Marion, Kelly, Andrew, Julia, Allan, Henda, Dan, Kate Ashton, Helen O'Connell, Katia Airola, Sharon Lambeek, Liz Biggin and many others.

Special thanks to Chris Collier and Geraldine Reardon for their valuable suggestions, and to Mirjam Zaat, Mary Daly, Paul Staal and Paul Robson, without whose help and encouragement this book would never have appeared.

One World Action

One World Action is a partnership between poor and exploited people in the South and those in the North who share their vision of a better, more equal world. We believe in taking bold, innovative steps to end poverty, inequality and discrimination, and support those who challenge the unequal distribution of the world's resources.

One World Action supports local organisations in Africa, Asia and Central America by giving money, goods, expertise and information as requested. We support community movements, women's and workers' organisations, cooperatives and small farmers' associations. What these groups have in common is a firm belief in democracy and equality linked with respect for human rights and freedoms.

One World Action has a programme of advocacy and education in Europe. We consider it a matter of urgency to bring to the attention of policy-makers and the public in Europe the concerns of our partner organisations in Southern countries.

One World Action, Weddel House, 13-14 West Smithfield, London EC1A 9HY
Tel 44 (0)171 329 8111, Fax 44 (0)171 329 6238, Email owa@gn.apc.org
Charity Registration Number: 1022298

Foreword

For some aid organisations, Angola is a 'complex emergency'. It is complicated and there are few ideas of how to deal with it. The usual responses of the outside sending food and other emergency supplies may not be appropriate, and may compound the problems caused by the over-optimistic advice of the outside world surrounding the elections in 1992.

This book attempts to show how people live in a 'complex emergency', how they attempt to build and maintain their own forms of organisation in these difficult circumstances, and how they can try to build on that.

Paul Robson,
One World Action

AFRICA

LUANDA

ANGOLA

Contents

ANGOLA

Introduction

It is not easy to convey the economic reality of a country where the rate of inflation is three per cent a day - in Luanda the capital of Angola, prices, including food, double almost every month. Nor is it easy to write about development in a country that has not had a lasting peace for 35 years and in 1996, as we write, knows only a fragile cease-fire.

But there is value in showing the rest of the world how Angolans living in poverty in the *musseques*, the shantytowns surrounding Luanda, survive the struggle against inflation and uncertain supplies of food, water and energy - in short, the struggle for life.

This book shows how people are helping themselves through the current crisis in Angola. It refers very little to events and decisions at the level of national or international politics, nor does it speculate about peace and possible postwar developments. In this sense, it reflects the feelings of most Angolans living around Luanda, whose main preoccupation is merely to get by from one day to the next.

Angola, Luanda and Ngola Kiluanje

Since 1961, Angola has endured one long destructive war. It began as an anticolonial struggle against the Portuguese and by 1975, the year of political independence, had turned into a war between liberation movements. Then, when South Africa began its armed raids into neighbouring countries, Angola became an international battlefield involving Cuba, the Soviet Union, the United States and Zaire. After the Cold War, the war in Angola persisted between the two remaining forces of the earlier liberation movements: Jonas Savimbi's UNITA and the multiparty government, dominated by the MPLA, the former communist party.

As a result of the Accord of Bicesse between the MPLA and UNITA in 1991, the economy was liberalised and free elections were promised. The elections were duly held in 1992 but, as readers familiar with Angola's recent history will recall, UNITA lost the elections and so returned to war.

In total, the United Nations estimates the death toll only during this period to be over half a million people, with more than two million displaced from their homes, 80,000 crippled and 50,000 orphaned. This is not taking into account the estimated half a million indirect deaths from hunger, malnutrition and preventable diseases caused by the warfare, mainly among children under five. Now, the country is on the brink of collapse, and the people are desperately looking for any form of recovery.

Yet this need not be the case. Angola possesses enormous riches: large reserves of oil and diamonds, good fishing grounds. It also has fertile land and a climate suitable for producing coffee and other valuable produce. But this wealth potential has not been available to the masses of people fleeing to Luanda since 1961.

Luanda is Angola's capital and largest city. It is also home to between two and a half or three million people - no one knows the exact figure. Because it is one of the few safe places left in Angola, the city's population has grown tenfold during the past 35 years, and by 20 per cent in the past three years alone. Yet, it has had almost no investment in infrastructure since 1975.

Ngola Kiluanje (named after an heroic Angolan King who fought against the Portuguese in the seventeenth century) is one of the communes that surround Luanda. It is made up of industrial sites and shantytowns, home to an unknown number of Luandans and migrants from all over the country. It is a place where the vast majority of people no longer have trust in politicians, neither in the government nor UNITA, the armed opposition. Both are fighting to make themselves master of Angola's rich natural inheritance.

Continuing inflation (2,000 per cent in 1995, 5,000 per cent in 1996) makes any investment, planning or savings by the people of this city impossible. The currency (Kwanza) was renamed once in 1990 to *Nova Kwanza* (at 1/1,000th of its former value) and *Kwanza Reajustada* (a further reduction to 1/1,000th) in 1995. (In this book we refer to the Angolan currency as the Kwanza, and prices as of August 1995 are based on an exchange rate of 6,000 Kwanzas to UK£1 or US$1.50.)

The results of the economic crisis are seen daily in this unfortunate city, and what is more important, the results are felt every day by its inhabitants.

How this book got started

I was introduced to Angola by Paul Staal, a Dutch consultant with a deep knowledge of the country. Together, we created the exhibition *Havemos de Voltar* (*We Have to Return*), before the elections in Angola in 1992.

When I made my second visit in 1992 I met Rui, a volunteer at an urban upgrading project in a Luandan shantytown. In 1993, I asked him if I could spend a weekend with his family in their house, which I had not yet visited. His reaction was one of total disbelief. To the knowledge of Rui and many others, a white visitor had never slept in the shantytowns, which are widely considered black strongholds and dangerous to strangers. But he agreed, and so I became acquainted with the family. During my visit, I became especially fond of Ricardo and Teresa, his father and mother and the heads of the family.

From this experience the idea arose to describe the development needs and potential of a city like Luanda from the point of view of its poorest inhabitants. Too often development policies and pro-grammes have the perspective of a helicopter, hovering over and looking down. I am convinced that working from the personal per-spective, which we have tried to take in this book, gives deeper insights.

In August and September 1995 a group, consisting of Alexia Gami-to, João Francisco da Silva, Pascoal Estevão, Vicente Albino Paulo (Genuíno), Jack Domingos Ramiro, and Victor Vunge was formed. Together we drew up a plan, divided the tasks, interviewed and photographed life in their shantytown - their *musseque*. Many in the group are new to journalism and this is their first product.

I wrote and edited the text of *A family of the musseque* in early 1996.

About the contents

In Chapter 1, 'The setting', we drive through Luanda, starting at the place where the first colonisers landed, a beautiful bay shielded from the sea by the peninsula called Ilha de Luanda. In an hour we arrive at the *musseque* called Ngola Kiluanje, where we meet the Ricardo family, who have lived in this area for almost 20 years.

In Chapter 2 we describe one day in the life of the people who live in the small enclosed compound, which is called a 'yard', owned by the Ricardo family. We become familiar with the central characters of the book and try to imagine what abstract concepts like *econo-my, development, war, democracy* and *gender* mean for the woman in the market and the man in the street in Luanda. Everywhere we look, we see people struggling, we feel the heat and smell the odours. With members of the family, we walk through the area, fol-lowing them through the economy in Chapter 3, their hopes for development in Chapter 4, local politics in Chapter 5, and the war in Chapter 6. In Chapter 7 we try to look into the future. In the epi-logue we ask the family and friends to speak again and to tell us what they dream for the future.

The 'day in the life' description in Chapter 2 is real, although it is not an actual day. It is a composite of typical routines and one not so typical event. We devised it from our notes taken over several weekdays in the Ricardos's yard. Each day we would take time out to write down what people did, how they reacted towards each other, where they were going if they left and where they came from when they returned. We also interviewed most members of the family - these are told as flashbacks in Chapter 2, or as highlights in the following chapters.

We are proud to be able to present this book, in which Angolan people, in their own words, express their feelings and show their daily life to non-Angolan readers.

Finally I, Bob van der Winden, must stress that I accept full responsibility for the contents of this book. The Angolan team delivered a huge amount of valuable material in the form of interviews, pictures and articles, but the final selection and editing of this material is my work. Therefore, all views expressed, including any errors and omissions are entirely my responsibility.

Luanda and Amsterdam, April 1996

Bob van der Winden, editor
Alexia Gamito
Jack Domingos Ramiro
Vicente Albino Paulo (Genuíno)
João Francisco da Silva
Pascoal Estevão
Victor Vunge

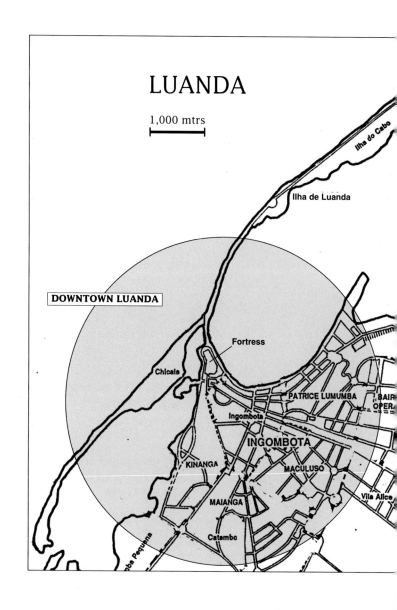

LUANDA

1,000 mtrs

Ilha do Cabo

Ilha de Luanda

DOWNTOWN LUANDA

Fortress

Chicala

PATRICE LUMUMBA

BAIR
OPER.

Ingombota

INGOMBOTA

KINANGA

MACULUSO

Vila Alice

MAIANGA

Catambo

mba Pequena

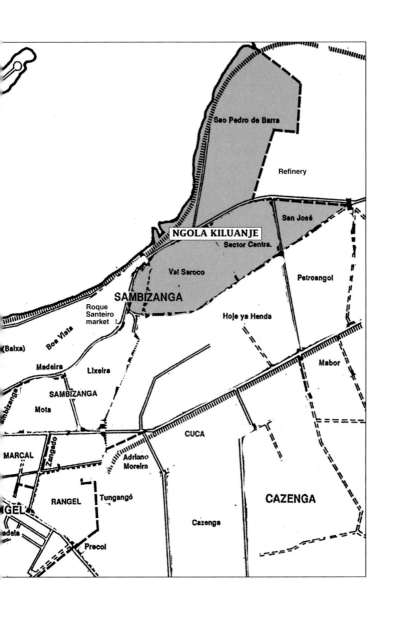

Chapter 1

The setting

It takes about an hour to drive from the beautifully formed natural bay and beach of Luanda, where so long ago the Portuguese and Dutch colonists landed, to the commune of Ngola Kiluanje. If we come ashore here, we see a boulevard, called the *Marginal*, lined with flats and offices along the seashore. On the other side of the bay is the *Ilha de Luanda*, the Luanda peninsula, stretching out to sea. The old fortress, built by the Portuguese in the fifteenth century and occupied briefly by the Dutch 150 years later, towers over the bay. During the weekends people come here to sunbathe and enjoy the nightlife.

We drive away from the shore and follow one of the narrow streets up the hill. In the city centre there are few potholes in the asphalt street, but the traffic is dense and many times we get stuck in a jam. Along the street, we see pleasant old Portuguese colonial buildings, alongside rundown blocks of flats. Most of these pretty buildings are owned by banks or government agencies - some have been restored and are used as offices. Some of the flats are very rundown - often the original owner left in 1975 and the present owners cannot maintain them - and we can see sewer water running down the walls.

Eventually we reach the limits of the old city and the road and the landscape begin to change. Potholes in the asphalt seem to be as numerous and haphazardly arranged as the buildings we now see around us - erected without reference to a plan or formal order. Big houses, surrounded by small corrugated iron shacks, and the occasional abandoned factory dominate the landscape. Amongst them, some formal buildings have been erected - an office for the 'administrator' (the un-elected mayor) of the Municipality of Sambizanga, police stations, fuel stations and the maternity hospital. People are everywhere: walking, sitting in the red sand along the roadside trying to sell some vegetables, or just standing. Children run alongside the car trying to sell whatever they might have.

Passing the market

As we near the enormous Roque Santeiro marketplace, now considered Angola's national market, the traffic jam worsens. Here, everything is for sale. Before the introduction of economic liberalisation and market deregulation in 1990, selling outside official channels was prohibited and this market was the heart of the *kandonga* - the unofficial market. Since then, it has become the norm. Although it will still take us another half hour by car to reach Ngola Kiluanje, this is where many people from that area earn their living. They buy and sell whatever goods are available; they cook for the masses of people who work at the market (the second largest in Africa); they sell their homemade bread rolls and cookies; or they buy things for resale at other markets, from their houses or even in other towns.

Fires burn on the heaps of rubbish - there are no sanitation services here - where old Portuguese sea-beacons tower over the market crowd. So much rubbish has been piled up around these beacons that these are the only places where erosion has not lowered the ground level - everywhere else it is two or three metres lower. This is the former city refuse dump and we can still smell it. The rubbish has only been partially removed and amongst the heaps of rubbish, people have erected tents where they find refuge against the burning sun or a rain shower.

Trucks, vans and cars are driving to and from the market on every possible square metre of the road, irrespective of rules or signs. Roving minibus taxis, called *kandongeiros,* sometimes packed with 30 people or more, drive haphazardly into the crowd and unload their passengers.

Sixty thousand vendors come here every morning, bringing all their goods with them. And every night they leave before sundown taking whatever they have not sold into the housing area, where they rent or own warehouse space. Everything passes twice a day over the one road that connects Sambizanga with downtown Luanda. Only the most courageous and armed vendors dare to stay with their goods in the marketplace overnight. Cruelly, one of the greatest threats comes from the police - the regular police, the traffic police, market inspectors and economic police - all of them are known to confiscate goods arbitrarily from vendors and customers. Even during the day, many people do not dare to go into the market, so we find people buying things inside and then trying to sell them along the road to the drivers of vehicles that pass at walking pace.

Entering Ngola Kiluanje

Now the traffic is getting less dense and there is less and less asphalt on the road. After three kilometres we have passed the market and enter the former industrial zone. Former, because only a few factories still function and the main source of income for inhabitants of Ngola Kiluanje is the market. The lorries of the old cement factory still stand where they were left in 1975 when a new factory was built further outside the city. The abandoned Lada garage (which functioned until 1990) still houses a few trucks - clearly it is no longer worthwhile to steal the carcasses - every removable part of them has already gone.

Now we drive over a small hill and see a big gasoline station on our right. To the left, a road leads to the sea and the harbour of Luanda. On our right, we can see the houses and shacks of the densely built neighbourhood: we are in Ngola Kiluanje, a commune of the Municipality of Sambizanga. To the left, we have access to one of the districts of Ngola Kiluanje: São Pedro de Barra, along the seashore where many fisherfolk live. The São Antonio church, run by Portuguese and German missionaries, is here, as is Luanda's jail: "it's easy to get in there, it's a miracle to get out again", people of the area are used to saying.

We drive alongside high concrete walls, now and then a watchtower on our left, patrolled by the military. This is Angola's only refinery and many times in the past a target of sabotage.

On the right, is the beginning of Val Saroco, a sector of Ngola Kiluanje. It is marked by a small marketplace serving the neighbourhood accompanied by small car repair shops, one of the many tyre repair stands in town, and small shops selling bottles of gas which they have bought from the refinery. Opposite the heavily guarded entrance to the refinery we turn right into Ngola Kiluanje.

Along the *Rua Direita de Ngola Kiluanje* - the main street of the district, between the oil refinery and the big Kwanzas Market - we find the Ngola Kiluanje Health Centre, which is also the main location of the Sambizanga Community Upgrading Project.

Bypassing the health centre, we head for the home of the Ricardo family, proceeding along the now better asphalt road, again bordered by heaps of rubbish. The road runs along huge warehouses where whole containers from the harbour are being unloaded and sold to the market women waiting in line outside. Today they sell imported secondhand clothing; women come here to buy a whole bale to be resold by the piece. We see a small bakery, a house in fact, in front of which Malik the baker is selling his cakes. We come across two schools, empty now because the morning shift of students and teachers has already left and the afternoon and evening shifts have not yet arrived. We pass the house of Mr. Sany, the biggest entrepreneur in the neighbourhood who owns several local businesses, including a bakery, a supermarket and a disco, as well as a restaurant in Cacuaco, a nearby seaside village.

We have to slow down for a police control but luckily we are waved through. On our left, we pass a group of women digging a trench, presumably to connect a water pipe to the main pipe under the road. Here we are at the end of our journey on asphalt roads, and the Ngola Kiluanje dusty dirt roads start as we turn right. The potholes have been filled with rubbish, waiting for a fresh layer of red earth. Very few cars come this way due to the rough driving conditions. In wet seasons it is almost impossible to drive through the mud. Because it is safer here than on the big asphalt road, children play with their buses and cars made from metal wire or old oil cans and run alongside passing cars, this time trying to get something from the white man.

Now and then a damaged *imbondeiro* (baobab) tree stands in the middle of the road, giving protection to a group of women sitting in its shadow, selling vegetables, cold drinks, beer, cigarettes, fish, cakes and so on from their small tables.

We pass a large rubbish-filled field, called 'Marconi' because of the many radio masts erected in it. On one side are Mr. Sanu's bakery and supermarket. After Marconi, in the middle of some houses, we pass the dirt field where the girls' football team trains daily. Then we drive through a maze of very narrow alleys, leading to the thousands of family yards where the 80,000 inhabitants of the area live. This is the commune of Ngola Kiluanje of the Municipality of Sambizanga, Luanda.

Arriving at the yard

Finally, after turning right at the *farmacia* (chemist) in the direction of the now abandoned truck garage, we drive up the hill and arrive at the yard of the Ricardo family.

The yard is approximately 30 x 25 metres, encircled by a wall of concrete blocks the height of an adult. In the yard there are six small one-story houses. In total, 14 adults and 20 children live here. Ten adults and 13 children belong to the Ricardo family, headed by *Ricardo Vieira* ('Pai', 56) and his wife *Teresa Fernandes* ('Mae', 47): *Fatima* (32) is their eldest daughter, living with *Ambrosio Pimentel*; they have three children: *Carlos* (7), *Maria* (3), and *Sadi*, who is just one year old.

Adriana, the second daughter, aged 30, lives in her parents' house with *Emilia* (9), her only daughter.

Rosa (29), the third daughter, also lives in her parents' house and she has five children: *Calolita* (12), *Mario* (10), *Gabriel* (7), *João* (4) and *Rui* (2).

José Afonso ('Zeca', 25), the Ricardos's eldest living son (his brother *Fernando*, who was a pilot in the army, disappeared in 1983) lives opposite his parents' house in the yard with his first wife, *Bernarda*, and their children, *Luciano* (4) and *Zinho* (2).

Angelina ('Lina'), Zeca's other wife, lives in the adjacent neighbourhood with one child, *Pedro*.

Mario Rodrigues ('Rui', 22) is the youngest son. He has been involved with *Linda* and has a child with her, but they do not live in the yard: *Miro* (5), Rui's son, visits his father during the weekends. Rui is now in love with Maria Santana, whom he hopes to marry.

Sandra (19) is the family's youngest daughter. She is in love with a young policeman, *Luis de Melo*. On the first of September 1995, the month of our visit, she gave birth to a son, *Bob Euclides*, now the youngest inhabitant of the yard.

Our story of one day in the life of this family begins with Fatima, the eldest daughter.

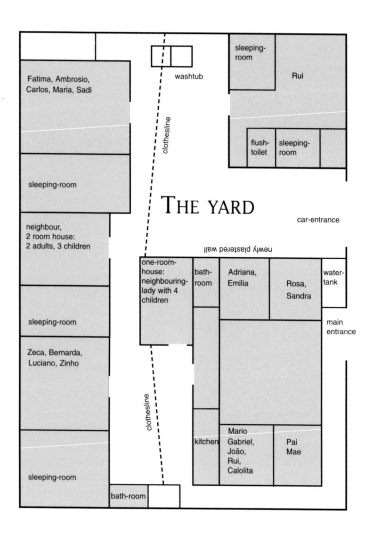

Fatima, Ambrosio,
Carlos, Maria, Sadi

sleeping-room

neighbour,
2 room house:
2 adults, 3 children

sleeping-room

Zeca, Bernarda,
Luciano, Zinho

sleeping-room

bath-room

clothesline

washtub

THE YARD

one-room-
house:
neighbouring-
lady with 4
children

bath-
room

kitchen

clothesline

sleeping-
room

Rui

flush-
toilet

sleeping-
room

car-entrance

newly plastered wall

Adriana,
Emilia

Rosa,
Sandra

water-
tank

main
entrance

Mario
Gabriel,
João,
Rui,
Calolita

Pai
Mae

Chapter 2

A day in the life of
the Ricardo family

Fatima is awakened every morning at half past five by the crowing of the cockerel, as the sun rises over the neighbourhood. During the night many leaves have fallen and it is her first task of the day to sweep the leaves and dirt from the yard's red sand floor. This red sand gives the shantytowns around Luanda their name: *musseque* (mu - place + seke - sand, in Kimbundu, a local African language).

After sweeping the yard, Fatima, with baby Sadi bound to her back, starts folding the children's clothes, which she washed the night before, and which have been hanging on one of the many lines running across the yard. Fatima washes the children's clothes every day, her own and Ambrosio's clothes are done on the weekend, when she washes the whole Sunday long, usually with her sister Rosa. When the clothes are folded she starts to heat some water on the coal fire to wash Carlos, her eldest son. School starts at seven for Carlos.

Fatima, the eldest child of Ricardo and Teresa, was born in 1963 in Pango Aluquem, a village 170 km (about six or seven hours drive) to the north east of Luanda. She lived in Pango until 1978 when she moved to Luanda, where she lived with her father's cousin, to continue her schooling. She finished the fourth grade of primary school but could not go farther in Pango. Her father and mother wanted to let her study, so when she was 15 she followed her older brother Fernando, who was already living in Luanda. Here she could continue her schooling and learn more than had been possible for her parents.

Pai

Fatima's father, Ricardo (called Pai by his family), had been fairly prosperous in Pango. He was a carpenter by profession and had always worked for the Portuguese priests, who lived on a small mission in Pango, as well as for other settlers. He also served as a carpenter in the Portuguese colonial army in Goa in India. But after two years he returned to Pango where he built a house for himself and the woman he married shortly after his return, Teresa Fernandes. In the first 20 years of their marriage they were able to build a beautiful house and accumulate a lot of land, which they have planted with coffee. They even had workers to take care of the crops. They sold the coffee in Luanda through the Portuguese landlords on the nearby big plantation.

By the time Fatima went to Luanda in 1978, Angola had been independent for about three years and Pai Ricardo feared that the Portuguese settlers might soon decide to leave Pango. And, the war, which had so far left Pango in the northeastern province of Bengo reasonably untouched, was getting nearer.

So Pai left his wife and the five younger children behind (Sandra, the youngest had just had her first birthday) and also moved to the city. He followed a two point plan: he took driving lessons so he could later buy a small car to bring his crops to town, and he bought a piece of land and started building a house in town. Today he is not very clear about his reasons for doing all this; sometimes he says it was for the education of the children, sometimes he says that he must have had a feeling about what was to come. Pai started building in that same year, on the very spot where Fatima is now putting the children's clothes in a plastic bag in the sleeping room of her two-roomed house.

Breakfast

With the noise of her work, Fatima wakes up Carlos, her seven-year old son, Maria her daughter of three, and Sadi the baby who was one yesterday. Ambrosio, her husband, is still half asleep and asks for coffee. But coffee is not ready yet so he turns over in bed.

Although Fatima owns a gas stove and makes a living selling gas bottles, she prefers to boil the water for morning coffee outside on a small cooking stove using wood or coal. The gas stove is in the living room because they do not have a separate kitchen. Fatima finds it quieter and faster to cook outside and this also saves her the use of expensive gas.

Fatima fills the stove with charcoal, sprinkles it with paraffin - in this yard paraffin is always freely available because Mae (Teresa, the mother of the family) sells it to the neighbourhood - and lights the stove. She heats the water in an old can and pours it into a cup with instant coffee.

Normally the family does not eat bread in the morning; they eat *funje* - cassava porridge - and drink coffee. The children drink water or sometimes milk made from imported milk powder, but not often because milk is expensive - 20,000 Kwanzas for one tin.

Never enough water

Now that Carlos and Maria are up, they have to be washed. Carlos first, because his school starts in half an hour. Carlos quickly swallows some cold porridge and some water. Meanwhile, Fatima picks up a bucket and starts filling the old iron washtub with water from the big tank. For this, she has to walk several times up and down to the big 5,000 litre water tank Pai built a few years ago. The tank is situated in front of the yard near the entrance, so that the tanker truck has easy access to it.

Since around 1988 there has been no pressure in the water pipe entering the yard from the main line. After independence, the amount of water, which is pumped into the system from the river, stayed the same - but demand multiplied. The entire capacity of the old system, which was constructed by the Portuguese, went to downtown Luanda. No more was left for the quickly expanding *musseques*, so today the area depends on water brought by tanker from the Bengo River, 20 km north of the city. For a few years the Sambizanga Project constructed public standpipes, but none were situated near the Ricardos's house. In any case, those standpipes have water only once in a while.

Although they do not like it, Carlos and Maria are washed in the chilly water. At the same time they hear their cousins Gabriel and Mario in another part of the yard, also being bathed by their mother Rosa, Fatima's younger sister.

Going to school

The children of the yard leave for school together, in their clean school uniforms, carrying their benches on their head. Schools have no money for furniture, notebooks or pencils. These four children go to school from 7:00 to 11:00 a.m.; then there is a shift from 11:00 a.m. to 3:00 p.m. followed by a shift from 3:00 p.m. to 7:00 p.m., at which time an evening class, mainly for adults, starts. So, all in all, this school has four shifts a day, in which it serves three groups of children and one of adults. Teachers normally work only one shift a day. Before 1988, there were only two shifts, but with the enormous influx of refugees from the rest of the country, this solution had to be adopted. The classes are full: at least 50 children per class is the rule; Carlos's school has 2,000 students in 10 classrooms.

Ambrosio

It is a quarter to seven now, slowly the sun rises over the brick wall on the eastern side of the yard, which separates the yard from the small alley behind the house leading to the Marconi field. Ambrosio got up a moment before and is on the old toilet, an old-fashioned latrine outside his house near the wall. He asks Fatima from there whether coffee is ready, and whether they will have bread or *funje* for breakfast. Fatima answers that she has had no time to buy bread. But Ambrosio can smell the fresh bread coming from the clay oven bakery just four houses from theirs and demands that Fatima go to buy him some. Fatima leaves the yard and goes to buy bread for her husband.

Fatima first met Ambrosio after she finished school in Luanda and was working as a secretary in a big state transport enterprise. She had finished the seventh grade and learned to type when she was 19. A year later, when she met him, Ambrosio was working as a photographer. When the couple decided to go to live together (they never married), Ambrosio and his brother divided the piece of land they owned into two yards and he and Fatima started making blocks to be able to build their own house later on. But then, in 1990, disaster struck: Ambrosio was arrested because a zealous policeman concluded that someone who owned a camera and all the equipment to develop and print photos had to be a spy. At the time there was an air of suspicion in Luanda because of the war (UNITA had recently attacked several cities again), but also because of the totalitarian state system. Meanwhile, his brother sold his piece of land and the policeman who arrested him ransacked his house and seized all his photographic material. Fatima had to pay a magistrate to have the film processed to prove there were no photographs of secret locations but only of weddings and birthdays, taken by Ambrosio in his work as a photographer.

While in jail, Ambrosio was severely beaten several times and had almost nothing to eat except the food Fatima was able to get delivered to him. If you do not bribe warders your husband could starve in jail, although it is only across the road.

Ambrosio was released three months later, after the magistrate took the trouble to look into the case, but still the policeman hunted him. Pai knew this and he decided the couple - Carlos was only two months old then - would be better off living in the family yard, so they obeyed and built a small annex to the old house.

The Futungo fields

While Fatima is getting the bread, the rest of the yard wakes up. Normally, Ricardo and Teresa are up early, but today they are not at home. Yesterday they went to the fields which they rent on the other side of town, near Futungo, the President's palace. Fatima also has a field there.

As Pai only earns a meagre 4,000 Kwanzas sickness benefit from his employer, the state coffee enterprise, the family has to survive in another way. A cooperative, mainly of inhabitants from this part of town, was formed and a small *fazenda* (farm) was rented from the Ministry of Agriculture. From the family, Mae, Pai and Fatima applied and were admitted. Now they rent a field 100 metres wide, and as deep as they want to work. It has become a real family place; many of the neighbours are nieces, aunts, cousins and uncles. Last year, they planted beans and cassava; now the beans have already been harvested, but the cassava needs more time - the roots will not be big enough until the end of the year. In the meantime, they can harvest the leaves to make *kizaka,* a traditional Angolan vegetable dish. This time of the year, the cassava fields need to be weeded and new fields prepared for the rainfall in December, by which time more beans and cassava will be planted. For this work, Pai, who has a lot of agricultural experience from the time in Pango, hires peasants who live near the fields, and he and Mae supervise. Fatima, and if necessary the other children, pay the workers and the transport costs. Yesterday, Pai and Mae went to the fields because the small van that provides transport was leaving with a lot of other people from the neighbourhood. Normally they stay in the fields for a few days. At first they lived in a grass hut with little or no cover from the rains, but Pai has since built a small house.

Men eat at the table

In the yard of Pai and Mae's house in Ngola Kiluanje, also live their daughters Adriana, with her nine-year old daughter Emilia; Rosa, with her five children; and Sandra who is pregnant and at the point of childbirth. They all awake between six and seven o'clock. Later, Rosa washes the older children first so they will be in time for school. Now she is washing the two younger ones and asks Fatima to bring her some bread too.

The house is small for so many people. Every 'family' has their own bedroom: Pai and Mae, Adriana and Emilia, and Sandra. Rosa and her five children also have only one room among all of them, but after Rui moved into the house he built in the yard, the three older children moved into Rui's old sleeping room. For all these 11 people, amidst all these sleeping rooms, there is one small sitting room with three old garden chairs and a table with four chairs. Usually, it is only Pai and Rui who sit there, but not often. Most often, the women and children sit in the kitchen or in the yard; and usually they eat apart from the men: men eat at the table, women in the kitchen, according to old Angolan customs.

Meanwhile, Calolita, who starts school at 11 o'clock, is pounding the cassava roots, which were soaked in water and dried in the sun yesterday. The flour she is making will be used for the family's lunch. After pounding the flour in the big mortar with a pole, she has to sieve it and pound the rest again until everything is sieved. This is a woman's job and usually Fatima does it, but the girls have to learn the skills of their mothers at a young age. Calolita also does most of the dish washing for the family. Calolita and Emilia, the eldest of the grand-daughters, are fully engaged in household work, apart from their school work.

When Fatima comes back with the bread (Adriana and Rui are now awake), Ambrosio is still waiting for his coffee, so she starts heating more water and pours it into a cup with instant coffee. Now even this family buys imported European instant coffee instead of the country's own produce. At one time, the family got coffee from Pai's work for Secafe, the state coffee organisation. But last year he developed health problems and had to leave. Pai's salary is still paid by the government, as sickness benefit, but it has not fully adapted to inflation. So, although the idea of sickness benefit is good, in practice it has little value.

Adriana

Adriana is grateful to her sister for bringing the bread as she is in a hurry. Today she has organised a driver with a van for herself and three colleagues, all of whom sell beer by the crate at the market. She is late now; normally she starts at the market at seven o'clock. The driver and the other women will be waiting for her to pick up her crates of empty bottles in the house where she rented some space for the night. During the morning she will go to the factory to buy 10 or more crates. If she is lucky, she will sell them the same day, but sometimes she does not arrive at the market with her load of beer until four o'clock. By then, it is too late to sell everything, which means that she has to sell the rest the following day. Adriana is by far the best saleswoman of the yard, but now the market is slow because it is the winter season - with temperatures around 10 degrees Celsius at night and 25 during the day. But in the hot months she sometimes sells up to 30 crates, making a profit of 70,000 Kwanzas a day. Adriana, who drank coffee while bathing Emilia, takes the bread her sister brought with her to the market.

Fatima

Now, after cleaning the house and the yard; folding the clothes; washing, clothing and feeding the children; and even preparing Ambrosio's coffee and breakfast, the time has come for Fatima to go to work.

As she is the only woman left in the yard, Sandra has to take over responsibility for the children. But she is still in bed, which is not usual for her. Fatima knocks on Sandra's door where she finds her younger sister sleeping. Knowing that Sandra is in her last month of pregnancy, she lets her sleep and tells Rui, her brother, to wake Sandra up when he leaves if no other adult is at home.

At last she can go to the refinery with her empty gas bottle, which she stores in the small tool shed next to the toilet. She puts the bottle on top of the cloth she wears on her head for this purpose and starts walking the kilometre to the refinery.

Next to the refinery are the shops where she buys the gas, which she then sells at the Kwanzas Market. The Kwanzas Market is not as big as Roque Santeiro, but houses an estimated 2,000 traders, wholesalers as well as retailers. A bottle of gas costs 17,000 Kwanzas in the shops. After walking two kilometres between the shop and the market with a full bottle on her head, and sometimes waiting more than four hours for a client, she can sell the bottle for an average of 24,000 Kwanzas. Some days she makes three of these journeys with an empty bottle to the refinery, and back with a bottle full of gas. But there are also days on which she waits all day with the full bottle, which she has to carry home unsold. Then the next day starts with a walk to the market with the full bottle, and so on. This is how Fatima makes her living, apart from the produce from the field she has in Futungo.

Fatima has many colleagues in the market: women like her, who buy and sell for small profits. The market is organised so that these gas vendors always stand on the same spot so that clients who come for gas can find them. All of them have their usual customers, people who prefer to buy from the same vendor. There is little competition normally, all the women here charge the same price. The one who sells a bottle is lucky and will be away for an hour or so, time for someone else to sell a bottle, and so it goes on. Nevertheless, the atmosphere in the market is congenial and there are always people to talk with. Fatima stands in a lively spot next to the cassava vendors, the fish mongers and a few men who have small shoe and watch repair shops.

Fatima has to do this kind of work because Ambrosio, like many men here, earns very little. Since 1992 he has not been able to travel to his parents in the small town of Piri, 250 km north of Luanda, to fetch food supplies. UNITA have occupied Piri and, although Ambrosio received a message that his parents were still alive, it is impossible for him to travel there or for them to come to Luanda. But even working as a photographer, he never earns much. These days he keeps chicken and ducks in the yard, selling the occasional one. Fatima is happy if he can earn enough for his lunches.

For Fatima, lunch at the market is usually just a bread roll with some cheese. Sometimes she cannot resist buying herself a good meal, but only if she has made a good profit that day. The food for an evening meal for the family costs around 10,000 Kwanzas, so for that she has to sell two bottles of gas. Moreover, she has to save some money every day so that she can buy tomorrow's gas bottle, bearing in mind the possibility that the price will go up again because of inflation or as a result of the government's structural adjustment programme. The last price increase was in gasoline, diesel, paraffin and gas. These prices rise every month on top of the rate of inflation so that, for example, a year ago a litre of fuel cost half a penny and today it is set at three pennies, tied to the currency exchange rate, which means a rise every day. (Compared to western prices, petrol is very cheap in Angola, but every rise hits the population very hard and in many ways; for example, as soon as petrol goes up, the bus fares are raised.)

Bernarda

After Fatima has sold her first bottle and is walking back to the market for the second time, she meets Bernarda, Zeca's first wife. Neither Bernarda nor Zeca have been sleeping in the yard at night so both of their children have been taken care of by Rosa and Sandra. Zeca has been sleeping with his other wife, Lina, in her house a few blocks away; and Bernarda has been to her parents in São Pedro de Barra, the adjacent district by the seashore. Bernarda's father is a fisherman and he provides Bernarda with cheap fish, which she sells at the market. That is how Bernarda earns a living. Whether she liked it or not, Zeca chose to take another wife while still living with her and the children. Sometimes, the only way for Bernarda to escape is to go back home to her parents for a few days, which she does every second week. There she helps with fishing and fish cleaning, just like before she became involved with Zeca.

Both women carry heavy loads, one a full gas bottle, the other a loaded dish of fish. They walk back to the market, chatting about Sandra's pregnancy and how soon they think the child will be born. As Sandra has been to the ante-natal clinics at the health centre, they know it will not be long to wait. Alarmed by their conversation, Fatima decides that as soon as she arrives at the market, she will send someone home to ask about her sister. So when they meet Rui in front of the health centre, where he works for the Sambizanga Project in the morning, they tell him they will be at the market during lunchtime and ask him to send them a message about Sandra when he goes home for lunch.

Rui

Rui, the youngest son, left home at eight o'clock this morning. As his neighbour, one of the two women Pai rents an apartment to in the yard, told him that she would stay home until lunchtime, he did not bother to wake up Sandra. Going to work, he walked through the small alleys, bordered by high old corrugated iron sheets or concrete walls, now and then talking with neighbours, most often because they wanted his help or advice. On his way, he passed the heaps of rubbish on the Marconi field and came to the main road. This is Rui's way to his morning job. In the afternoon, he teaches the third class at São Pedro de Barra. In the morning he works for the Sambizanga Project, which rents a small office in the health centre. When the Sambizanga Project started in 1987 it organised mainly health actions, helping the health centre to get equipment and medicine - the doctors and nurses were still paid by the government. It also organised house-to-house visits of young volunteers from the neighbourhood who had been especially trained for this purpose: to give information about common illnesses, and advice on vaccinations and hygiene. But since then it has developed much further, constructing public water standpipes in the neighbourhood and initiating a dry pit latrine programme, where people can get the materials to build their own latrine.

Rui was one of the first Sambizanga Project volunteers, or *activistas,* as they are called in the project. He had also participated in *Amigos do meio Ambiente* - 'Friends of the Environment', a group of young activists organised around rubbish cleaning, tree planting, organising parties for children and so on. Now that he has finished his studies, he manages the new Local Initiatives Fund for the Sambizanga Project in the morning, as well as teaching in the afternoon. With this fund, he has set up 20 small projects with a maximum of UK£300 each, monitoring each to see if the money was spent according to the stated goals of the project. Projects range from latrines for the market through to shirts for the girls' football team, to materials for entire classrooms of the secondary school. You can do a lot with UK£300 in Luanda!

By the time Rui arrives at the Sambizanga Project office at around half past eight, there are usually people already waiting for him. As soon as the rumour of the fund had begun to spread, all kinds of people became interested in applying for it. There are no other funds available in the area, either from the government or non-governmental organisations (NGOs). Among the applicants there is a remarkable number of good, serious projects, but just too many to be supported. Rui shares the office with Dona Orquidea, who has been the coordinator of the project in the area since 1987. This means he can discuss the applications with an older and more experienced person. But even with this help it is an enormous responsibility for a 22 year old.

Lunchtime

After work Rui usually walks back to his house again, where he either has lunch with his father; or, if his father is not home, alone in his own house. Rui does not cook. He has no gas in his new house because he lives alone with no woman to cook for him. He still depends on his mother's kitchen, where sisters Sandra, Rosa and Adriana do the cooking. As Rosa and Adriana work in the market and only cook in the evening, the cooking for lunch (which, in Angola, is usually a hot meal) is generally done by Sandra. Then, all the children who come back from school around noon, eat in the yard, Sandra in the kitchen with Mae if she is not in the field, and Rui with Pai at the table.

But not today! When Rui enters the house, little Calolita tells him that Sandra is still in bed, in pain, and has just told her to go fetch her mother. Rui tells her to do this and goes into Sandra's room. At first he does not know what to do - to him this is women's business. But a moment later he realises that he is the only adult in the yard. Sandra is sure that it is now time to give birth to the baby, and that she may have to go to the maternity centre in Sambizanga, nearer to town. Quickly, Rui decides to send children to find more people: one to an experienced aunt living nearby, to assist at the birth, and another to find Rosa, who is also experienced in pregnancy and births.

But Fatima arrives first, still carrying a gas bottle on her head. Greatly relieved to see her, Rui leaves them together and goes to see if he can get a project car and driver to take Sandra to the maternity centre. He walks all the way back to the health centre, where he finds Euclides, one of the Development Workshop drivers, with his white land rover. By radio telephone, Euclides obtains permission to help Rui and together they drive back to the house.

More than an hour has passed by the time they reach the house, and by now all the women have arrived. It takes some time to find and load into the car everything the maternity centre requests patients to bring with them: clean water in tanks, aseptic gauze, bandages, clean clothes and so on. Sandra is in pain but she manages to get into the car. Finally, with the car fully loaded, they leave: a family of one brother, three sisters - of whom one is about to give birth - and an aunt.

A sudden birth

Although everyone and everything is now in the car, they have a difficult trip ahead. The roads in the *musseque*, especially near the Ricardo yard, were not constructed for cars and overuse has created big potholes and deep trenches, making the ride slow and uncomfortable but manageable nevertheless. Euclides drives as fast as he can over the dusty roads, constantly manoeuvring to find the smoothest way, trying not to harm Sandra and the baby.

All in all, this is not an easy time for someone at the point of giving birth. Sandra, in pain, lies half on the floor, half on the benches of the land rover, covered with cloths and supported by her sisters and aunt, while Rui sits in the front of the car. Now and then she moans softly, and the women encourage her to have patience and wait until they reach the maternity clinic.

When they arrive at the main road, they meet the never-ending traffic jam around Roque Santeiro market. It is impossible to proceed with any speed: the traffic is so dense and creeping forward so slowly that it takes them half an hour to move one kilometre. Having been distracted by the traffic problems, the driver and passengers are startled by a sudden sharp cry from Sandra and, coming from under the cloths, the cries of a baby. Despite the surprise, there is no panic in the car; the women catch the baby and support it underneath the cloths, allowing nothing to be revealed to the men in the car.

Now that the baby has emerged, the older women, without hesitation, decide that there is no need to pay for the clinic and that it would be best to go back home. As they are starting off, Rui suddenly realises that they are quite near the house of his girlfriend, Maria Santana. So they turn around and head there, saving mother and half-born child another gruelling and dangerous half hour over the dusty roads without medical help.

At Maria's house, the women lift Sandra and the baby out of the car, still managing to keep them both covered. Many curious women gather around and mother and baby are laid on the floor of the sleeping room, the umbilical cord between them. Meanwhile, Rui is sent with the car to the health centre to find a nurse to help with the afterbirth.

Half an hour later they return, finding everyone still in the same place, but now for the first time the men can see the naked baby lying on cloths on the floor, and to their joy it is a boy. Fortunately, Samuel Kialanda, the nurse accompanying Rui is experienced. He expertly cuts the umbilical cord, helps with the afterbirth, which comes smoothly, and takes the baby, proudly held by Aunt Maria, back with him to the health centre. Here the baby is weighed, registered and vaccinated by the greatly relieved staff of the health centre, who of course all know Rui and his sister. With the baby, they drive back to the main road again and pick up Sandra and her sisters to bring everyone back home.

Throughout all this, Rui and Euclides had necessary and supportive roles to play, and they did these well. But at all times they kept a discrete distance from Sandra and the birth. This is, after all, strictly women's business and men should have as little to do with it as possible. Male nurses like Samuel are accepted in some urban areas where the people have become accustomed to the idea. This is not to say that men in the family do not have other responsibilities, for according to Angolan custom it is the family of the father that has the prerogative to name the first born, especially if it is a boy. Nevertheless, it was some time later before anyone thought to tell the baby's father, Luis de Melo, although he lives nearby.

Preparing for the celebration

Home at last, the mother and newborn are put in Sandra's own room; her sisters bathe the baby, wash Sandra and clothe them with the clean clothes that were packed to take to the clinic. Relief is felt by everyone, especially for Sandra, for whom this seems like the greatest event of all time. Just then, Fatima remembers that Mae and Pai ('the old ones', as she expresses it) are still at the Futungo fields and will probably not return before the weekend, because of the lack of transport. Euclides, the driver who has been helping all afternoon, is begged to make another trip of two and a half hours to pick up the family's founding couple so that they can celebrate the birth of their new, still unnamed, grandchild. As expected, Euclides agrees, and he sets off with Fatima and Rui for Futungo; they will not return until after dark.

For the time being, Rosa is in charge and she has to establish order. The daily routine has been thoroughly upset: the children who normally go to the afternoon shift at school stayed home, Rui had to abandon his class at São Pedro de Barra, the other adults also only worked for part of the day, no food was bought, Sandra was not able to cook and Mae was not here to take the lead. And still, no trace of the baby's young father can be found, so Rosa sends one of the children to at least tell the other grandmother of the birth.

Ambrosio arrives home to find he can now take his first picture of the day, although, of course, not one he will be paid for. This brother-in-law's pleasure at the birth also prompts him to offer one of his prized ducks for the evening meal. The offer is quickly accepted and so the day which saw the birth of a new child is to be celebrated with a feast provided by an adoring uncle.

Having missed their lunch, everyone in the yard is very hungry so all effort is directed towards getting the meal ready. Emilia buys bread rolls at the market, and preparation of the duck is led by Rosa. The effort is assisted by the arrival of Adriana, at her usual time of five o'clock. She is astonished to hear all that has being happening while she was waiting at the beer factory for her turn to buy 10 crates. Immediately, she begins to help by buying food, taking care of the little ones and preparing the room to welcome the neighbours who will most certainly be coming. By now, the news has already spread through the area and, according to Angolan custom, they will come to give money to the mother and child to ensure a prosperous life for the newborn.

Meanwhile, Aunt Maria teaches Calolita and Emilia how to behead and pluck a duck, and a real meal is prepared, awaiting the arrival of Pai and Mae.

Zeca

Just before dark, Zeca arrives from his work. He heard the news in the small projects' workshop at Vale Saroco, where he had been to organise the delivery of food aid to his group of displaced people. The displaced live all around the area and come mainly from the northern provinces. Employed by a 'food for work' programme, Zeca manages a group of 74 *deslocados* (displaced) who are working on the roads in the area. This is an innovation for the neighbourhood: they clean up old rubbish heaps, fill the deep potholes in the roads with decayed rubbish and cover the whole road with a new layer of red sand. So the roads are improved while, at the same time, the very unhealthy rubbish dumps all over the area are gradually removed. Zeca works with six groups, everyone working seven hours a day, who are paid with 35 kilos of food a week, one for every hour of work. Today they have covered the first part of the third road they were working on. Content with the advance they had made, the group had gathered, late in the afternoon, in the small workshop to pick up their food for the week. It was there that José, the foreman, told Zeca the news about his sister.

So Zeca came home, walking as fast as he could, sweating and cursing because of the load of food he was carrying. But despite all this annoyance, the eldest brother of the family was very happy with the new family member, his youngest sister's first son.

Together at last and happy but for the sad memories

It is six o'clock, and darkness has fallen. Zeca and Ambrosio go into their houses to look for oil lanterns. This is the only lighting they have during the night, apart from the coal fires on which the women cook, and around which the family members sometimes gather. Some, like Rui, own battery torches but batteries are very expensive. Two years ago the transformer, which supplies this area with electrical power, broke down, and it still has not been repaired, leaving 10,000 people without energy. Like the water problem, the city's electricity company has no means of repairing broken transformers; and if they had the means, these would be allocated to downtown Luanda and not to the *musseques*. This means no television and no radio, except for a battery radio belonging to Rui. But more importantly, lack of electricity also means that they cannot run their refrigerators and freezers, and so they cannot earn from selling ice lollies in summer, and it is impossible to make small savings by buying large quantities of food, like cheap fish and meat, and storing it for a long time. Complaints to the authorities have failed time after time. A group of people once collected a large sum of money for improvements but these never materialised, and the money disappeared.

So, gathered around the fire, the yard lit by oil lanterns, is how Pai and Mae find the family when they return. Of course, Mae is the first one to visit Sandra in her room and to admire the new baby, surrounded by neighbours who come and go in a steady stream.

With the arrival of Pai and Mae, and with almost every member of the family present, it is at last time to start eating. The men begin by gathering around the fire, while the women sit with Sandra and the sleeping baby on the bed. Here they talk about what happened during the day, and how lucky they are to live together in the family, as in old times back in Pango. The older women recall that, in similar circumstances, one of the neighbours had lost her daughter who was giving birth to her first baby.

Outside, Pai Ricardo remembers the times he sat around the fire with Fernando, his eldest son. Now he wonders if Fernando is still alive, or if he died after his disappearance. Nobody has heard of him since 1983, just before he vanished with his MPLA fighter plane, and later when he was broadcasting on Radio Vorgan, UNITA's radio transmitter. It is still not known whether he defected from the MPLA or was captured and forced to talk on the radio for UNITA. Everyone had hoped to see him in 1991, after the first peace accord, but he did not show up and there has not been any news from him. Even after so many years, Pai is deeply affected by thoughts of his missing son, and it is at happy family events such as tonight's that he feels them most keenly.

Chapter 3

The *musseque* economy is a women's economy

For the average poor Angolan, Angola's economy is one of survival - a 'buy and sell' economy. This applies to millions of poor Angolan citizens, whether they live in the countryside or, like the Ricardos, in the *musseques* in town.

Apart from the Ricardos, we questioned many other women, all of whom estimated the cost of one meal for an average family of six people at 10,000 to 15,000 Kwanzas. This is quite understandable, comparing the market prices with a daily food ration. For one week, a family of six must raise a minimum of 140,000 Kwanzas for two meals a day, no breakfast. Per person, this is 25,000 Kwanzas a week, in money or in goods. And this amount rises every day as many prices are directly linked to the exchange rate. The daily inflation rate is one thing every Angolan citizen understands. The prices mentioned here are as of August 1995; one month later they will have doubled.

Inflation makes it impossible for people to save; not even to put away a part of their salary or earnings to buy food later in the month, unless they take the loss of changing their money into dollars for granted. There are many people who change dollars on the street and the more or less official 'change offices' are booming. Nevertheless, for most people inflation is the worst part of the crisis: it makes salaries earned in the formal economy a cruel joke because they are not doubled every month to keep pace with inflation.

So at the end of 1995 the Kwanza was worth 1/21 of what it was at the start of the year, while inflation in 1996 was even higher - up to 5,000%.

How to survive

How does the Ricardo family cope with this inflationary crisis? How do they manage to survive under these circumstances?

Speaking in terms of averages, the Ricardo family is not rich. There is no money for luxuries, additional housing, or housing improvements. Except for Rui and Adriana, no one has been able to (re)build their house or invest; all their money is spent in daily food expenses. No one in the family (except Zeca) drinks beer or wine, or soft drinks or even milk. They do not usually eat meat, do not go out for leisure (except Zeca) and work most of the time. If they eat chicken or duck it is one they have raised themselves and they consider it a real luxury. Only the women eat at the market - but no full meals, only something simple like a bread roll.

On average, the women earn the most and spend the least on themselves. Ambrosio and especially Zeca spend most of the money they earn outside the family. In this respect, Pai Ricardo and Rui are exceptions: many Angolan men take little care of their wives and children. However you look at it, this family's economy is not only a survival and 'trade and bargain' economy, but is also a women's economy.

Inflation rate
UK£1 on the parallel exchange market is worth:

January 1995	2,000
February 1995	3,000
April 1995	3,500
May 1995	4,000
June 1995	5,000
August 1995	6,000
September 1995	8,500
October 1995	15,000
November 1995	30,000
December 1995	42,500

Market prices

rice:	3,000 a kilo
fish:	5,000 a kilo
fuba, cassava meal:	1,500
bombom, untreated cassava:	15,000 a bucket
tomatoes:	four for 1,000
other vegetables:	average 3,000 a kilo
onions:	1,000 each
garlic:	500 the 5 bulbs
peanuts:	6,000 a kilo
bread:	1,000 a loaf
cooking oil:	12,000 a litre
sugar:	6,000 a kilo
beans:	5,000 a kilo
maize:	1,000 a kilo
meat:	20,000 a kilo
milk powder :	20,000 a tin
sausages:	25,000 a tin
butter:	12,000 a tin
water *(from the tanker)*:	1,000 a bucket
beer or soft drink:	3,000 a bottle
wine *(one bottle)*:	5,000, at least
gas:	22,000
(one bottle lasts around half a month)	
paraffin *(5 litres)*:	4,000
second hand clothes: average	5,000 a piece
one ride with the *kandongeiro*:	1,000
one concrete building block:	1,000
one 50 kilo bag of cement:	19,000

(6,000 Kwanzas = UK£1 (US$1.50) August 1995)

The currency was changed in July 1995 and the name was changed to *Kwanza Reajustada*, 1,000 times the value of the former *Nova Kwanza*. For reasons of simplicity we adjusted the exchange rates throughout the year to the value of the *Kwanza Reajustada*.

The Ricardo family income

Pai Ricardo gets 4,000 Kwanzas (about 80 UK pence) a month sickness benefit from Secafe, plus the rent of two rooms (5,500 Kwanzas) and the income from the field in Futungo, which earns perhaps an average of 200,000 Kwanzas a month in food (sold or consumed). Mae sells lamp oil (paraffin) and makes an average profit of 3,000 for a five litre jar, totalling perhaps 25,000 a month, she also has a field in Futungo, earning her another 200,000.

Fatima earns an average of 6,000 per gas bottle, making around 200,000 a month. She is the third person in the family to have a field in the cooperative, estimated to earn 200,000.

Ambrosio has no substantial income from photography and has been cut off by the war from his parents in Piri, from where he no longer gets any food, but sometimes he sells a chicken or duck, earning about 10,000 a month. Adriana is the best saleswoman of the house. She earns between 30,000 and 70,000 a day, an average of one million a month. Rosa sells whatever she can sell, she says she earns around 200,000 a month. Zeca has his income from the Sambizanga Project (53,000); but the food he gets there has far more value: eight litres of cooking oil, 25 kilos of beans, 22 kilos of rice, 50 kilos of maize: together an estimated 350,000 a month. Bernarda, his first wife, sells fish that is subsidised by a low price from her father who is a fisherman. According to Zeca, she earns around 200,000 a month. So this family unit earns 600,000 altogether.

Lina, Zeca's other wife, who does not live in the yard, sells second hand clothing which is a 'real earner', says Zeca, but we will not count this in the family income, as Lina supports herself and her own son with it, only marginally assisted by Zeca with a part of the food supplies he earns from the project.

Rui is the one who earns most in the formal economy: 30,000 at school and 75,000 in the Sambizanga Project (NGO salaries are more or less related to the exchange rate). On top of this, he earns some money now and then from an organisation or a school if he helps them organise the building, for instance. Let's say this adds up to 150,000 in all, but he also gets the same ration of food as Zeca: 350,000 a month, which makes 500,000 altogether.

Sandra has no income of her own but she is of tremendous value to the family as she is in charge of all the children in the yard (around 20 in total) during the day, cooks the hot lunch for the children and all adults who are home, and does the shopping and a lot of cooking at night. In short, she is the family's 'housekeeper', organising the household of the whole yard.

Total income of the Ricardo family, average per month in thousands of Kwanzas	
Pai	210
Mae	225
Fatima	400
Ambrosio	10
Adriana	1,000
Rosa	200
Zeca and Bernarda	600
Rui	500
Sandra	—
Total:	**3,145** thousand (3,145,000) Kwanzas a month
	UK£525 *(exchange rate August 1995)*

Of the total monthly cash income of 3,145,000 Kwanzas, only 160,000, around five per cent, is earned in the formal economy, and of that, only 10,000 in the Angolan formal economy, 150,000 being salary from Development Workshop and paid by foreign donors. An estimated 600,000 (18 per cent) is agricultural produce from the Futungo fields, 700,000 (22 per cent) is food aid ('food for work'), and the other 55 per cent is earned by the women in the informal economy.

So, against a rate of 6,000 Kwanzas for UK£1 (August 1995), this family earns a monthly income of UK£525 for 10 adults and 13 children. Of course, one year later, by the time this book is printed, these incomes will be at least tenfold but as we are comparing them with prices and exchange rates from the same month they give a good impression.

Compared to *musseque* standards, this family is pretty well off. They fear no hunger, although this might not be the case without the earned food aid, or if the fields fail to produce due to the occasional drought. Their children go to school, and they are clothed, although their clothes are old. You could even describe them as middle class, but their relative prosperity is only due to the organisation within the family that allows people to work day and night, and to the money the women earn in the informal economy, which is more than half the family income.

The women in the market

These results, based on interviews with the family, agree with data compiled by Henda Ducados Pinto de Andrade, one of the few economists studying this subject. She works for the 'Luanda women small enterprise project' of Development Workshop.

"It is better to speak of the economy of 'the woman in the market' than that of the 'man in the street', if you talk about the economy of the *musseque*. The secret of the economy is called *compra e venda* - buy and sell. Apparently, the Angolan state income from oil and diamond revenues allows many goods to be imported from abroad. The unofficial *kandonga* system that replaced the rigidly controlled 'socialist' economy pre-1990 allows all kinds of people, especially women, to buy small or even larger quantities of imported goods, to sell them in smaller quantities and make a small profit. This is usually just enough to buy the food for the day, although some women make higher profits. This is the most common face of the informal economy of the *musseque.*"

Talking about her project for market women she continues: "Our project is, in the first place, a research project: nobody knows exactly who the actors are in this process and what the main difficulties are. The project will also develop a training programme and study feasible interventions to support women operating in the informal sector. We also try to establish a women's network of various local organisations interested in development and gender in Angola. This includes integrating government agencies; we want to make the government more aware of the sector, in order to develop policies to support it."

Angola state income at a glance

Angola's economy has always been interrelated with that of the wider world. Before being colonised by the Portuguese, Angola exported slaves and ivory. During Portuguese rule, it exported agricultural crops, diamonds and iron. Around 1970, oil overtook the other products as the main income. It is mainly produced offshore and in the northern enclave of Cabinda. By then, this principal income did not stay in Angola but went to private bank accounts in Portugal and elsewhere abroad.

The country did not develop and most 'luxury items' were bought abroad with revenue from oil and diamonds. After independence, economic collapse was caused by war damage, mismanagement, forced collectivisation and corruption.

In this respect, there is little difference between the warring parties. Looking at it schematically, in terms of natural resources, the war is fought on the basis of the income from oil on one side and diamonds on the other.

Nevertheless, the estimated state income of seven to 10 billion dollars a year from oil and diamonds provides imported food for the cities, mainly Luanda, although most of it is spent on warfare. The rest of the country is left to produce their own food on a subsistence base. It is estimated, that a quarter of the national income is spent abroad to buy food for the cities. It is this food that ends up at the market, sometimes sold and resold four or five times.

Different kinds of buying and selling

The Ricardo family women are not the only women selling goods along the streets. Some women sell from their homes in small stalls at the door, usually looked after by one of the older children. Some can be found in small square-like spaces *(praçitas)* in the midst of houses, where between two and 10 women sit in groups behind their stalls.

Then there are the larger markets, such as the Praça Coragem (the 'market of the brave' - so named because cars pass very nearby on the road and have caused casualties), where around 100 to 200 hawkers are active, the Kwanzas Market (we could not find out whether it had been named after the river, the province, or the currency) and the largest of them all, further away along the shore - the Roque Santeiro with its 60,000 vendors, the majority women - which we passed on our way from downtown Luanda to our neighbourhood in Chapter 1.

It would be an understatement simply to say that buying and selling is the most important survival mechanism in Angola at the moment. So we asked some of the women about their trade and they explained how they work.

Lisa Antonio

Dona Lisa lives right behind the Ngola Kiluanje Health Centre in a small alley, where she and other women in the street sit behind their tables, waiting for customers. She lives with her husband and nine children. Her husband does not work; he has a licence to sell charcoal, but since there are no trucks coming in from the provinces there is not much work for him these days. Her eldest daughter works as a teacher and earns 25,000 Kwanzas. So, Lisa is responsible for the main family income:

"I sell cigarettes, peanuts, sweets, and wine. I buy them at the Kwanzas Market or at the Roque Santeiro. I make most of my profits selling wine; normally I buy a crate of wine every day. I buy it at 5,000 a crate and sell the bottles one by one, to make a profit of 2,000 a day. The same goes for a kilo of peanuts, which also makes me a profit of 2,000 a day.
I have no idea how much profit I make in a month, we live by the day! But I know that I can only make two meals a day regularly; breakfast and the evening meal. Only if business is good I can make lunch for me and my husband. Nevertheless, the children eat something after they come back from school, so they have three meals a day, even if sometimes it is only cassava porridge."

Eduarda Santana

In the small market, called *tira o sapato* (take off your shoe), five alleys away from the health centre, in the direction of the field where the radio masts stand, we meet Dona Eduarda.

She lives in a household of 16 people with her father and mother, brothers and sisters. Two men work in the cement factory (Cimangol) and bring in a salary, her mother still has three small farms not far outside the city: in Funda, Panguila and Porto Kipiri. There, she stays a month or two and afterwards she brings the crops to Luanda to sell them at the Roque Santeiro market. Nowadays her mother saves the family from starving. She cultivates beans, peanuts, sugar cane and many other crops. Eduarda helps her with harvesting in September and with selling in October. During the rest of the year:

"I sell spaghetti, cooking oil, tinned milk, sausages, butter, sugar, and anything else that is available. I also buy water from the tanker and sell it out of my home tank. I buy my goods at Roque Santeiro market and sell them here; I come here every day, and stay here with the merchandise until two o'clock in the afternoon. Then I see what I need, go to Roque Santeiro and buy things in order to sell them the next day. I have many clients, it's like a small grocery shop, my mother's sales in October give me the possibility to buy larger quantities of goods. If I sell them and buy new goods with a small profit we can just make enough to make the new harvest next year. I can't explain to you how hard it is at the moment, but I can tell you, that if we had the opportunity we would travel abroad to flee from hunger. But we have no money to travel, so we're stuck here."

Sandra Francisco

Moving along the asphalt road from the refinery, alongside the health centre, we arrive at the Kwanzas Market. Here, wholesalers, like Adriana Ricardo, sell goods such as beer by the crate or wheat flour by the bag. The general public also come here to buy from retailers like Fatima Ricardo and Sandra Francisco:

"I buy cassava by the bag at the Kwanzas Market. It costs me 120,000 Kwanzas. Then I sell it by the bucket for 15,000. This results in a profit of 10,000 to 25,000 Kwanzas a day, just enough to buy food, but there are also days when I don't earn a penny. We can't cope with this inflation: every day prices rise, not only of imported luxury goods, but food prices. It's the government that always makes things more expensive; they raise the price of petrol, and everything becomes more expensive. The dollar rises and straight away the food prices rise. There are many people who have no money to trade, so there's nothing else left for them but stealing. We hope that soon the roads will open. At the moment it's impossible to travel into the interior and that makes food expensive. Even now there is a formal cease-fire and yet people who try to find food out-side of the city are dying. We want peace, we want to be able to go where we want, we want to work on our fields to grow food in order to sell it."

The reason we find so many women trading this way dates from 1990, when the economy was deregulated. These days people can-

not live on their salary from the formal sector and the informal sector is the only way to survive. Thus, most families are headed by women, in terms of income. Men working in the formal sector cannot sustain their families financially on their own. Also, because of the war, a typical 'nuclear family' in the district is composed of seven or eight adults plus any number of children. Many refugees

from the provinces, where the war has generally been worse, have sought refuge with their families living in Luanda.

This family pressure forces women to struggle in order to make ends meet, and one of the ways is engaging in micro-economic activities. Normally, women try to get together some finance, perhaps the husband's last salary, or some family savings. Sometimes an informal loan from friends or family helps to start buying and selling for a small profit at the market. If they succeed, it is barely enough to buy some food, and the next day they have to start all over again. They have no external help from development NGOs or government to expand their activities. Nor is it generally possible for them to produce any type of goods because they lack raw materials and credit.

Before, market women had a system for savings of their own, known

as the *xixikila* system, in which every day a group of women paid
a fixed amount to one member of the group. So, for example, in a
group of 20, every 20 days you would have a larger sum that allowed
you to buy more goods to sell or things you need for the family.
Unfortunately, due to inflation, this has stopped. People simply do
not have enough money to buy themselves food, let alone to save.
There is also a universal decline in living standards. People who had
running water in their houses now have to buy it from the tankers,
entire communities no longer have electricity, people only eat two
meals a day, and there are people who have not bought clothes for
four years. The Angolan economy is in severe crisis, and it is felt
harder in Luanda because this is where people have been fleeing to
for the past 20 years, and at an even higher rate since the resumption of war in 1992.

Development of small trade

Sometimes you also see men working at the market, but 75 per cent of traders are women. Men do not sell food, but mainly goods such as spare car parts. They also perform a useful trading function by travelling into the country, now that roads have opened up a little with the cease-fire. Women cannot travel because they have to take care of the children and feed the family, work that is rarely done by men. If people have a place in rural areas from where they can get food, perhaps the small farm where they come from, it is not uncommon for men to travel there and back and for women to sell the produce at the market in Luanda.

Conversely, people also buy commodities at Roque Santeiro, and take them to sell in provinces like Moxico, or to the diamond area, where the prices are higher, thus making bigger profits. You will also find women coming from the provinces selling their vegetables. They bring in a certain amount and try to sell it in one day at the market but may sleep there if it is not sold, staying until they have sold what they brought.

Although most of the economy of the *musseques* is based in the informal sector, it is fraught with many practical and commercial difficulties. Many women have few skills and little knowledge of their rights. Furthermore, they get no support and feel isolated. For example, vendors don't understand record keeping or cash flow. They cannot make a profit and loss analysis, they do not know how to develop their business, or how to make a simple business plan. They do not market their products by advertising and they do not organise themselves collectively in order to obtain better wholesale prices from the importers, and so on.

The informal economy could play a major role in the reconstruction of the Angolan economy, after peace has truly been established. With some improvements, it can absorb more workers and so it might even provide employment for demobilised soldiers. And what is of direct importance for the women involved in it at the moment is that it can bring higher profits and also higher levels of overall employment for the same capital input. What is necessary for this to happen is a raising of consciousness and a development of skills, not only among the women involved, but also among government agencies and NGOs.

Women can be challenged to develop their enterprises and to raise the value-added of their products and generate better surpluses. The informal system already provides most of Luanda with food from the provinces against high risks and costs. It could become the backbone of a wholesale and retail system to feed the city after return to more normal post-war circumstances.

Tina da Cunha
"I sell the fish that my husband brings from Benguela. He owns a car and travels with it to Baia Farta. Although it's dangerous - many people have died on that route - we have no alternative to earn a

*living. We have lived here for two years now with my sister and my
four year old daughter in a house of two rooms, for which we pay
50,000 rent a month. Only if there is peace will we move back to
Benguela to cultivate the land again and do better business. When
we arrived here in Luanda things were better, but they are deteriorating every day. Especially because prices are rising sky high.
Also, with our business and our car we do not earn much more than
55,000 a day. And we spend at least 30,000 of it on food, but we
also have to buy water, soap, save for medicine if we get ill, the rent
and so on. How can we possibly live?
We could travel to Benguela, but there is a lot of banditry along the
road, they kill people 'just like that'. The very government policemen, who should protect us, request 50,000 Kwanzas to let us travel in peace. If you don't give it, they simply take everything including
your clothes. Or they might even kill you. The ones that should
defend you are those that do you most harm at the moment!"*

Pyramid system

The trading system is very complicated and, in fact, similar to the
European trading system, only at a much lower and also distorted
scale. There are also absolutely no regulations, so the largest profits are made by the strongest and the wealthiest entrepreneurs,
and the state controllers and policemen frequently do not protect
the small vendors, but on the contrary they earn from their plight.
A good example is the flour trade. The 'selling circle' works as fol-
lows: wheat flour is imported by someone with a line of credit or
capital of their own. That means that it arrives, usually from Europe,
in big white bags of 50 kilos each in one or more containers on a
boat. Once the container is out of customs, the flour goes to the
warehouse, from where it is sold. For flour, there seems to be a
monopoly; in any case, the price seems to be fixed if people buy it
from the warehouse. The market women go to the warehouse as
soon as they know it has got flour. Their operating margins are
very low, one per cent at most, but there are two types of women
selling at the market. First the wholesalers, with more buying power;

they might even sell up to twenty bags at once at the market, and never less than one bag. And, there are the retailers who only buy one bag and sell the flour by the cup, usually a coffee cup.

On all levels, there is an enormous need to organise the women, especially so that they can protect themselves against unscrupulous suppliers and harassing police. Until this happens, most profits will be made at the top of the pyramid, where a few importers have been able to obtain import licences from the government and manage to change their money at a favourable exchange rate. So they import cheaply, but sell at the prices of the parallel market.

Henda Ducados Pinto de Andrade: "This is also due to the transitional period we still live in: since 1991 the economy has been moving away from centralised planning towards a market economy. But since the war resumed in 1992, no coherent economic programme has been implemented. So the government promotes a market economy, but the still existing and never abolished legislation from the time of centralisation has impeded its development. It is in this vacuum, that (sometimes foreign) big traders can obtain licences from corrupt government services and make profits over the heads of the simple Angolan traders at a lower level in the pyramid."

The warehouse: Fernando Neto

Along the main road between the health centre and the Kwanzas Market, we find various warehouses. Two of them, opposite the police control post, were burned at the end of 1992 as an act of retaliation. The owner was known as a UNITA supporter and after the fight for control of Luanda, an important part of which was fought out on this very road, people looted the warehouses and burnt them down.

But further on, we find some warehouses still functioning, where women stand in line, waiting for their turn to buy second hand clothes, batteries, televisions, chocolates, soft drinks, furniture or mattresses. They are owned by a Portuguese syndicate and they sell their products wholesale or sometimes retail. The goods come from various countries: Hong Kong, South Africa and elsewhere in Africa.

We talk with the manager, a 30 year old man who is also studying at the Faculty of Natural Science, Fernando Neto:

"We have many clients. What is especially difficult for them is the constant change of the exchange rate. We import goods from abroad, and have to charge them according to the price of the dollar. But we can see that the market cannot cope with the rise of the dollar. Sometimes people come here to ask about the price of the goods and then they come the next day to buy it, but in the meantime the price has become too high for them.

We cope with inflation ourselves by cooperating with a change office. Every day we deliver our money there and they change for us and keep a percentage. We have little stock in the warehouse at the moment, because there are three containers stuck in the harbour; there are always a lot of formalities. Also, the boat from South Africa is always late, and that also causes delays.

I hope that there will be peace and our country can produce for our own needs again. As it is now, everything is imported and all prices are related to the dollar. We should be able to produce fruit juice here, which we now import from South Africa. That's the only way to stop inflation as we have it at the moment. We have had the Kwanza, the New Kwanza and now we have the Readjusted Kwanza, and none of them is worth the paper it's printed on!"

Bakeries

Bakeries are among the more productive segments of the *musseque* economy. Baking bread is now the most widespread informal micro business in the *musseque*; the profit is even enough to live on for a day.

The small shop owners that bake bread in their homes, or in their little bakeries, mainly buy one bag of flour at a time, and produce around 500 bread rolls from it.

Actually, flour and sugar are the best things to sell at the moment; everyone eats bread here and it is the most affordable food item. A little bread roll costs about 500 Kwanzas in the *musseques*; in the bakeries in town it costs double that. A loaf of bread costs 1,000 in the *musseque*.

The informal bakeries make bread called *pão burro* - donkey's bread.

It is usually made in a back yard or living room, most often in an ancient type of wood-burning oven made of bricks or mud. Bread in town is made under more hygienic conditions in more sophisticated ovens, which is why it is more expensive.

Manuela and Malik's bakery

"We came from Kaxito, directly after the elections of 1992, when we had to flee from there because the war arrived. We have family here in Luanda, and now we live in my sister's house. We left Kaxito with virtually nothing, no clothes, no food, no money. So we had to start all over again when we arrived here. In Kaxito I worked in the military as a supply officer, let's say as a military salesman. That provided us with a small pension once we were here - 3,000 Kwanzas. And this amount has never gone up with inflation, that's the way things go here. But in those days we still could save some of it, also thanks to our family who helped us a lot. So it became possible to buy the oven.

When we had at last saved enough, we had no money to buy the flour, we even didn't have money to eat. But the family helped us so we didn't starve. You know we wanted to start this business so much, and we had to struggle so hard for it, that all kinds of people helped us. Once we had enough material, the gas, the flour, the milk, the cooking oil, the yeast, the sugar and the butter, we were helped enormously by a friend of mine, who taught us how to make these cakes, the very cakes that we're still producing. That's the way we learned how to produce the cakes.

Fortunately, many people started to praise the quality of my cakes and the amount of cakes sold increased all the time. Then we started to give credit to the women who sold the cakes; we didn't request payment in advance, but let them pay when they had sold the cakes. That way, we got more people working with us. At the moment, we produce 500 cakes a day. At one time, we even finished a bag of flour in one or two days; now business is less, and we use one bag a week. The people have very little to spend at the moment; it's already difficult for them to buy bread, let alone cakes. Also, there are a lot more cakes at the market than before; last year we were one of the few who baked cakes, now there are many more bakeries of this kind. And the prices of my materials are also high. So sometimes we spend a lot of money on the materials and we earn only a *little bit. Normally, we start working at eight thirty in the morning, we start baking at nine thirty and we work altogether three hours to bake one trough of paste. Then we wait to see how fast we sell these cakes. Sometimes we bake another half or a whole trough, but only if we've sold enough. Our customers are the retailers: the women who pick up their cakes here and go selling them at the nearby markets or in the streets. The moment they've taken away all the cakes, we're free. This way we earn around 20,000 a day.*

Nowadays I can buy flour in the warehouse, because the prices are low and they've plenty of flour. Before, nobody wanted to sell you just one bag; they only help you for 20 bags or more at a time. The warehouses normally buy it from abroad. Our brand is called Tiger, I don't know where it comes from, maybe even from England."

Chances for development of Ngola Kiluanje

It is extremely difficult to foresee what the future development of all this enterprise might be. But a few observations can be made for the area, and even the whole of Luanda. In the first place, and most important of all, women are the pivot on which the whole enterprise system turns.

In the second place, it is of great concern that the overall level of vocational training in Luanda is the lowest known of all African cities. And women, especially, lack any kind of training.

In the third place, the tax and licensing system is incomprehensible to most people, especially the untrained. This, and fear of the market police, prevents women from upgrading and formalising their business. In any case, they can see that the system does not work: none of the women interviewed have ever paid taxes, nor have they even thought of it, and licences are only necessary higher up in the pyramid.

In the fourth place, inflation and the war cause so many obstacles for any kind of development that only in time of peace and reduced inflation is it possible and worthwhile for women traders to invest in their businesses.

The reasons behind this are obvious. The growth of Luanda from half a million to nearly three million inhabitants over the past 20 years means that the majority of urban dwellers came from the country with little or no schooling. The need for better training is felt by many Angolans. All women try to send their children to school, at least until the sixth grade. If you ask them, they see the lack of training and education as a great impediment to further development.

Furthermore, Angola's economy has never developed much beyond mining, oil and (in the past) agriculture. This is, of course, to a great extent due to the Portuguese economic system, which was in place until 1975. However, the socialist system that followed contributed very little to people's self-reliance.

Ambrosio, Fatima's husband, expresses it this way: "Before the war came to Piri, around 1985, my father didn't work his coffee fields, he earned something as a tailor. We didn't produce much, because the coffee had little value inside the country. You could not sell it, only barter existed. So you exchanged it for a bit of soap or sugar. Anyway, historically, Angolans have always produced just the amount that was necessary for their own consumption. People were not interested in production because you only supported the government with it, or, better said, certain people inside it. But if this changes and after the war real liberty of trade develops we will certainly produce more."

In the long term, it is of immense importance whether today's vendors in the street will regain trust in the government or not. If the feelings you hear expressed by many saleswomen, such as: "thieves or murderers, all these politicians are the same", continue, not many people will invest in their business. With today's state of the economy, where large oil and diamond revenues are used to buy arms or 'consumer' goods by the government and UNITA, 'the woman in the market' has little alternative but to play her role at the bottom of the trading pyramid.

But there are a few bright spots, even in Ngola Kiluanje. One is the presence of a few modern businessmen in the area, who might form a focal point for development in the near future. Mr Sany, a local businessman, is their spokesman. The second is of course the presence of so many women who have had the obligation, but by this also the opportunity, to get involved in trading. With the help of the new women's project they are a big source of future development.

Mr. Sany

"I am a businessman, living along the Main Road of Ngola Kiluanje. My organisation, 'Sany', is a trading organisation; we work in import and export, trade and industry. We own a supermarket here in the neighbourhood, an industrial bakery, a disco, two bars and two ice cream shops. We started here more than two years ago. We face several difficulties here, especially caused by the war: the government cannot fulfil all its plans to improve the economy because of the necessity to defend the country. But nevertheless it has been possible to obtain credit from the bank, although the interest rate is 210 per cent. But if we take into account that the inflation is even higher, this doesn't worry us very much.

It is indeed very difficult to overcome the problem of inflation; only with the greatest efforts and using all our skills we can manage. During the period of 1985 to 1995, thousands of entrepreneurs here in Angola collapsed because of this inflation.

Of course, many of them were only 'fly by nights' and we are different: we invest in the real infrastructure of the organisation, we invest in machinery and that is what the bank needs when they decide about credit.

64

As far as the bread is concerned, this is - as anywhere in the world - a first necessity product. Everyone at least tries to have breakfast and we are the only bakery here in the area, the central sector, which has 100,000 inhabitants. This is, of course, one of the main reasons for my establishment here in Ngola Kiluanje. I like it here, I can work well, I live well, besides here I am far away from all the competition in downtown Luanda, where there are many shops.

We all know that life is very difficult in Luanda at the moment, also in the district here people suffer a lot. I would like more merchants like me to get involved in the district. The population will only benefit from it. We are not interested in making fast profits and then leaving, as some of my foreign colleagues might do: they're not even interested in painting the wall, they are merely passing. We think that the people here deserve more, so we also did a few things for the neighbourhood, according to our possibilities. Of course, we know that some development organisations have done work for the water standpipes and so on. I think, that things will go better from now on.

For instance, you can see that there are many people here in the area who sell products, let's say they are some kind of 'makeshift supermarkets'. I am certainly prepared to try to help quite a few of them with small credits. In the framework of our developing as wholesaler, I can even imagine restructuring my supermarket to a full wholesale organisation. Especially since the nationally operating enterprises are closed for these people. I could even use quite a few colleagues 'up here', on our level of the pyramid. There ought to be more big enterprises to help to develop the area this way. It's a shame, that, for instance, the refinery, who is our neighbour doesn't contribute at all to the area, while we run the risk that there might be an explosion. They have never done anything, nothing for the roads, neither for the street lamps.

It really is a general problem: the people here are all out of funds; people lower their consumption - there are families who bought 20 loaves of bread before, and now buy two. We need peace, a lasting peace. We need implementation of the peace accord. Luanda is jam-packed, it's impossible to develop it as full as it is now, people have to be helped to return to their villages once there is peace. Then we can start. I prefer starting in practice; I am no theoretician, I don't like plans, I want to see results. And it is generally known that many people, also here in the district, have beautiful plans, but they have to fulfil them!"

Development of the women's project

The success of the bakeries - where a lot more value is added to the flour than by merely reselling it - sparked off a willingness among women to develop their skills under the women who were involved in the urban upgrading projects of Development Workshop. On the basis of such needs, Henda Ducados Pinto de Andrade developed the Women's Enterprise Development Project:

"The training we do here for women focuses on improving the current management and business skills of the participants. Our aim is not to introduce new skills; instead, we are more inclined to study extensively the actual practice. Starting from that, we'll try to improve it bit by bit. Many women have, for instance, no idea about their rights, so it is easy for policemen to harass them.

It is also very tiring to sell in the market and to do the whole work for the family.

There are very few agencies who do work in this field. The Ministry of Planning and Economy, together with UNDP, have elaborated a five year plan to support small businesses in the formal sector, but they asked us to develop the informal sector. We will be working on a manual for trainers to help them in the field. Also AAD, a local NGO, is supporting the informal sector with credit and raw material.

But the credit part was not very successful, mainly because of the incredible inflation of 20 per cent a week. We will be looking for a better way to organise credit schemes. We intend to do this by elaborating that with the women themselves so that they can define what the main problems are. We will also study it in practice by giving credit to the participating women, and we will try to make recommendations to local government and banks. We believe that the informal economy, especially in the peri-urban areas, can mean a lot more for the population than it does now and we will most certainly try to spark off initiatives at a national level."

Indeed, there is great willingness on the part of women to improve their skills, which sometimes they have learned just through experience, and to develop their enterprises. When asked, one of them indicates that she would like to become a fishmonger, another would like to build up her ambulant selling to a real shop, others might step up the ladder and become traders, bringing in food from outside of town. Quite a few are interested in starting their own bakery or food store, or improving their cooking at the market, towards something that looks more like a restaurant or a 'luncheonette', as they call it. Maybe even some of them will get higher up the pyramid and start small wholesale enterprises in certain commodities. Women like Adriana, one of Pai and Mae Ricardo's daughters, who is already selling beer by the crate, certainly have the talent for it.

Adriana Ricardo

"I start working at seven, first I go downtown, to Sao Paulo, to one of the beer factories to buy a number of crates, usually between 10 and 30, depending on the season. I pick up the empty bottles first and together with a few other women we hire a car to bring the crates to the factory. We buy for around 40,000 Kwanzas a crate and we sell the crate for 45,000 to 50,000 at the market. So I make a profit of around 5,000 a crate, costs of transport deducted. I only sell full crates; my clients sell the bottles from their homes, in their luncheonettes or at the market, cooled for consumption most of the time.

My job involves a lot of 'trade money'; we don't get any credit from the factory. Sometimes they even request us to pay in dollars! On the other hand, I have to give credit to some faithful customers; but if they order beforehand, they pay half of the crate's price.

It is a lot of trouble to get the beer; most of the time I stand waiting in line from eight to around eleven o'clock, so I don't arrive at the market before twelve. Sometimes, one of the beer factories doesn't

sell at all, so you have to go on to another one, and hope that you can get some beer there. Fortunately, there are a lot of customers waiting for me then. The crates that I don't sell before five o'clock are stored in a house near the market.

I have a seller's licence. You pay for it every year. They're not expensive but it costs a lot of trouble and money just to get them. But now I have one. Taxes are low. Police check my licence sometimes because the name of the licence has to be filled in on the invoice from the beer factory. But as I give them a couple of beers once in a while they're my friends.

Once I'm home I start cleaning the yard and the house. The children, who are alone during the day, make a big mess. And also the men never clean up anything. Sandra cooks in the afternoon, so we cook the evening's dinner with three women: one day Rosa, one day Mae, and I cook the third day. The men don't cook; they pay for the food now and then, like Rui, who does a lot for the family, but they don't cook. Many times men don't even pay for their family, so I feel better without one."

Chapter 4

A 'do-it-yourself' neighbourhood

Luanda, Angola's capital, is also its oldest city, founded in 1575. It is situated on the Atlantic coast, in a semi-arid region (400 mm of annual rainfall, concentrated in three months) and covering an area of 2,000 square kilometres. It has the status of a province and consists of nine municipalities and 24 communes.

Luanda was originally a European-style city, in the mode of the Portuguese invaders. The difference between European downtown Luanda and the African shantytown districts, the *musseques*, is stark.

At the time of writing, Luanda's inhabitants number an estimated two and a half to three million. The growth of the city during recent decades has been spectacular. The following data illustrate the soaring rate of growth:

1818-	4,490 inhabitants
1881-	11,172
1930-	50,588
1940-	61,028
1950-	141,647
1960-	224,540
1974-	590,000
1983-	934,881
1990-	1,590,000
1994-	2,500,000

Compared with the country's overall population, Luanda is becoming far more concentrated. In 1960 4.7 per cent of the population lived in the city, in 1983 12 per cent, and in 1990 25 per cent.

Today, an estimated 30 per cent of Angola's population lives in Luanda.

The main problem is that the last urban planning dates from 1975, when the population was a mere 550,000. The steady influx from rural areas, mainly due to the ongoing war, combined with an almost total absence of city planning, has resulted in an overburdening of the existing infrastructure and a steep decline in services for the city's inhabitants.

Filipe Colaço, Professor in Demographics, described the situation to us: "I'm very concerned about Luanda's future. An enormous migration (70 per cent of the population of the city are recent immigrants), a birth rate in the order of 56 per thousand and an average birth rate of eight children per woman, makes me foresee a suffocated Luanda in the coming decades, in physical as well as social respects. Projections into the future might bring us to expect a population of five million in 2010 or 2015.

The actual disastrous situation will only turn out to be a faint shadow of what is awaiting us: lack of drinking water, lack of electricity, sewer water running over the streets, lack of housing, schools, hospitals, jammed traffic, more crime and deforestation."

Refugees from the war

Still, migration continues into the city, where food arrives more easily and people hope to find better conditions for survival. In Luanda more than 60 per cent of the population is estimated to have migrated directly or indirectly because of the long war that has raged in the country.

Some of the refugees have been lodged in enormous camps in the outskirts of town: on the road to the north - to Kaxito, for instance, 50,000 people still live in tents. But most people fled to members of their family who already had a house in one of the *musseques*;

this was the case of Manuela and Malik, the bakers who live in an improvised house in their family's yard.

Sometimes refugees, like Domingos Tunga who works in Zeca Ricardo's rubbish removal project, built themselves shelters on pieces of 'no-man's land' between other houses.

Domingos Tunga

"I live in the area called Cimangola, after the cement factory. I arrived here in 1987 from Moxico province, from Luena. I worked as a driver then and was on my way back when the road to Moxico was attacked by the enemy. It was an ambush of UNITA, that burned 17 cars. Seven people died. We were driving in a convoy with the army when UNITA attacked. The cars that were not damaged drove back and they took me. When I came here in '87 I started working on a truck, and I made quite a few trips to Uige, Nambwangongo, Mbanza Congo and other places in the interior, so I made a lot of friends over there. Then when the war broke out in those regions, I began to see them all coming here to Luanda, and many of them live in Cimangola now. The area filled up in '92, after the last war started. Before, there were not so many people.

I work here as chief of the second shift in the rubbish removal project. I live near my uncle's house in my own dwelling. My uncle is a clergyman and so he has possibilities to help. My house has only one room, made only from iron sheets. I live there alone. I have no money to rent a real house! My daughter lives in her own house. Sometimes I don't eat because I'm living alone. If I come home late, and if there is no water in the nearby tank, I go to sleep. I have no strength any more to go to a distant water tank to buy water. But sometimes I cook for myself: *fuba*, meat, rice.

Here in the project they pay me with eight litres of oil, and beans, maize, rice to a total of 22 kilos, and sometimes I sell some of the food to buy other things. I like it here in the project, anyway it's the only place to find work, and I survive on the food; but if the possibility arose, I would certainly accept another job, like as a driver."

Waves of migration

In general, three major waves of migrants can be discerned. The first wave came directly after 1974/75 when the MPLA had established their power in Luanda, but while the war was being fought fiercely outside the city. Pai Ricardo was in this wave when he arrived in 1978 from the province of Bengo.

Over the years, migration continued steadily but a second wave arrived just after 1985, when US President Reagan began to support UNITA with US$30 million of armaments a year. Domingos Tunga arrived then. As he says in his testimony, the Cimangol cement factory area where he now lives was still quite empty then, but filled up after 1992.

The third and largest wave arrived after the 500 days of peace in 1991 and 1992. In this wave, many people from the provincial capitals of Angola fled to Luanda. This was the first time that big cities of several hundreds of thousands were besieged or occupied by UNITA and is the main reason for the enormous influx into Luanda in recent years.

Lourenço Jacinto and Antonio Ernesto
Lourenço Jacinto is a neighbour of Domingos Tunga, having built his house next to the cement factory: "I fled from Mbanza Congo when UNITA took the city and killed two of my friends just because they had been part of the election committee. Under UNITA I can't go back there for sure, but also after the government takes it back, I won't move. I don't want to lose everything again. I came back from Zaire and moved to Mbanza Congo after the Bicesse treaty in 1991. We thought peace was here to stay. But now I am here, I don't even know where my parents are.
Since coming here I have had a job with my uncle. I'm a driver of a

kandongeiro so I do have some income that allows me to build my house little by little, and I am not giving it up again!"

Antonio Ernesto, who lives in a refugee camp outside the city: "We fled from Cacuso, 150 km from Luanda, walking through the fields and woods, after UNITA took back the village for the second time. Each time it was conquered by UNITA or the government they shot at random at a lot of villagers who they believed belonged to the other party. Hundreds and hundreds of people were killed. At first we stayed with family in the musseques, but they cannot support us. Now we are trying to build up this camp. We are 5,000 people right now, and we hope to return to where we came from. But the land mines keep many people here."

Building around the factories

Building in Ngola Kiluanje started long before independence in 1975. At the beginning of the 1960s the area was designated as an industrial zone. The refinery was built, and around it related indus-

tries sprung up along the road from downtown Luanda to the small village of Cacuaco on the seashore and to Kaxito 50 km north of Luanda.

Around the factories, workers, who mainly came from outside of town, started to build their houses. Before 1975, the Sambizanga central area, which is closer to downtown, was already a densely populated area and known as a revolutionary stronghold. In the actual Ngola Kiluanje area, dwelling areas that were organised like neighbourhoods existed only around the main factories like the refinery, the cement factory and the *Tecnocarro*, the truck workshop.

Just before independence and especially after it, the large and steady influx of newcomers from the provinces and areas further away began. The growth has mainly affected the poor areas, the *musseques* like Ngola Kiluanje, where there was still space between the factories to build your own house. People who arrived from the provinces, like the Ricardo family, were used to building their own houses so they did the same in Ngola Kiluanje. They bought, rented or occupied a piece of land and started building without much formal planning or organisation. Neither before independence nor afterwards did any municipal authority, neither the colonial nor the revolutionary, have the intention or means to impose a structure or organisation on the people's self-building.

No regulations

Pai Ricardo explains: "When I arrived in Luanda in 1978 with the intention of starting to build a house before things got worse in Pango, I began looking for a building site in the neighbourhood of my nephew's house, located opposite the refinery. I wanted to buy a piece of land, and through my family I heard that a Mr. Sourdo who has a business near the place where all the butchers of Luanda used to dump the bones of the slaughtered beasts, called *Bairo dos Ossos*, had something on offer. When I first got it, the land was twice as large as I'm living on now, because while I was away for some time in 1979 other people arrived and occupied it, as it hadn't been fenced yet. It has stayed that way ever since. When I bought it there were only trees here, and it was green all over. This is a good piece of land because it is more or less on top of the hill and catches the occasional breeze. I already knew a lot about building, being a carpenter, and I learned bricklaying and did everything myself with the help of Fatima and Adriana, my daughters. Imagine, a bag of cement cost 250 Kwanzas in those days, now it costs 25,000 Kwanzas! In those days there was still water in the main water pipes so we could make a connection. Water was cheap then. Now you pay 2,000 Kwanzas for a 200 litre barrel from a tanker, there is no water in the system any more."

Fifteen years later, with the help of his father, Rui Ricardo also built a pleasant looking house. Not everyone in Ngola Kiluanje has such a good dwelling. Some people have never had the opportunity to invest and still live in a timber house, a *pau a pique* - wooden poles bound together. António João is one of these. He came here 37 years ago from Kaxito, in the province of Bengo, and was one of the first to start building here, while he was employed by the truck workshop. But he has been jobless since 1980 and so he has not had enough money to improve his house.

People who arrived in later waves built all kinds of structures, more or less pleasing to the eye, more or less temporary, and generally covered with corrugated iron or concrete roofing sheets. Most of the houses are made from concrete blocks, around 20 per cent are constructed of timber.

So there are many variations within the *musseques*. If you enter a yard, usually separated from the alleys by old corrugated iron sheets, you might find a beautiful oasis with plants and green trees, but you might just as likely find a yard containing heaps of rubbish and open latrines.

The houses and yards have one thing in common: people have always built them themselves, only sometimes helped by hired labourers. No street plan or building regulation, or any public construction programme has ever been imposed by any government, local or otherwise. Only in the relatively distant past, around 1980, did the revolutionary government subsidise prices of building materials to give people the chance to build for themselves.

Building a house

Rui Ricardo built his own house on his father's land: "Fortunately, I could build in my father's yard. There is no more space in the area and I would have had to go too far away, in the direction of Cacuaco. Building does not only depend on money, but also on skills. My father knows a lot about building and he guided me. For instance, he explained to me that the foundations are very important; in the rainy season, houses with bad foundations are in danger of deteriorating quickly, because the water enters the house and into the foundations.

I'm not quite clear about the full cost of the house. You know, here in town people start saving for a house by buying concrete blocks, little by little, when they have the money. It's better to save blocks than money with the inflation we have here. So I saved materials and built my house over three years.

At the moment, a concrete building block costs between one and one and a half thousand Kwanzas. But we made them ourselves for around a quarter of the price. We only bought the water and the cement. The first bags of cement cost me 2,500 Kwanzas, now you pay 25,000 Kwanzas. I was lucky that I could buy the roofing sheets all together for 87,000 Kwanzas a year ago. Now I would not have the money to buy them. For the things I could not do I've hired a specialist, for instance, for electricity and the plastering of the outer walls. Unfortunately, I haven't had much pleasure from the electricity lines and lamps I installed. For two years we have had no power at all in the whole neighbourhood.

My father urged me to build a really good house at once. If it had been just up to me, I would have built a smaller house, because this house has really caused me a severe headache. It has four small sleeping rooms, a central living room, a kitchen and a toilet and has nine by five metres surface area - 45 square metres.

If I make a guess, the house cost me two and a half million Kwanzas in cement (UK£416). The roofing sheets cost me an estimated UK£140. So all together, I invested around UK£700 in the house. I haven't spent very much these years apart from the materials for the house. I bought the chairs for UK£30, the cupboard cost me UK£26 second hand, I only had to buy new glass for it. The table and the five chairs around it were 750,000 Kwanzas recently, so that was UK£125. Now I don't buy any more furniture - it wouldn't fit in the living room.

I prefer to save some money if I can, I would like to buy another building site, if the possibility is there; living here in the yard with the family is a good thing in these difficult times, but in time of peace it would be less complicated to live on my own grounds!"

Talking about development

In an area like Ngola Kiluanje, people do not expect big infrastructure projects. If you ask them about 'development', they speak of small scale improvements, organised and carried out by the people themselves. Their goals for improvement are much more basic and immediate:

"The greatest problem of the area is that there is no water. And in large areas, like where we live, there isn't any electricity either. With water and electricity life would be a lot better. Then I could make ice lollies or sell cold drinks. But for two years we have had no electricity here, and no government institution is doing anything about it!"*(Fatima Ricardo)*

"I cannot tell you how difficult it is. I would have liked, at least, to have a somewhat better house, so that my children could have a slightly better home. I would like to give my children a future, especially let them study. But all I see is that things get worse day after day ...." *(Lisa António)*

"We have big problems with banditry. They break into your house while you're asleep. We cannot sleep quietly. Police should do their work instead of robbing people themselves."*(Eduarda Santana)*

"What I think is the worst problem of the area is the roads. They're full of potholes and rubbish. You can't even come here by car." *(Ambrosio Pimentel)*

"I would like to have water in my yard, and repair my house. And I long for peace so I can travel to my home town again." *(Maria Rodriguez)*

"Apart from the things we're already working on, there is the lack of electricity that bothers me. And there is no room for people to amuse themselves, no space to play football or baseball, or for discotheques." *(Zeca Ricardo)*

Well, this last wish might be fulfilled in the near future:

"As far as my own business plans are concerned, I hope to open a restaurant and discotheque next to the supermarket next year, with a satellite antenna for television, air conditioning, etcetera. And I will start a project for a *pastelaria* here, where people can buy their cakes for birthdays, etcetera." And, jokingly: "I even see possibilities to open a clinic here in the area, maybe I'll buy the health centre!" *(Mr. Sany)*

Clearly, these are goals that many would see as developmental, and in this respect there is no great difference from the defined goals of, let's say, the World Bank and other big donors. The real difference lies in how the projects are executed. People in the *musseque* are used to helping themselves, they have done so for decades, even in the most difficult circumstances. They are pretty well able to develop their own surroundings with a little help, and they do not expect huge infrastructures to be built for them. On the contrary, any development that has not been implemented with the people has been doomed to failure, even if it is only indifference to the maintenance, a condition that quickly leads to the decay of any donated infrastructure, as many examples prove.

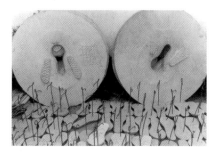

Self-help improvements

People have always helped themselves as far as their own housing is concerned, and the Sambizanga Project demonstrates that with a little bit of help, infrastructure can also be improved this way. The following cases illustrate this point.

House-to-house visits by young activists identified problems and gave information, about the health centre, for example.

Households were supplied with chlorine and later all water tankers bringing water into the city were chlorinated.

A building workshop, which now operates under Angolan management, was installed in nearby Cacuaco. Later, a smaller mini workshop was built in Vale Saroco.

The dry pit latrine project was introduced for people to buy the latrine slab and other materials at reduced prices.

Public water standpipes were built and connected with the main incoming pipeline, so that more people could use the scarce water coming from the municipal system.

From time to time, clean-up campaigns are organised to burn rubbish in the streets, now extended to the 'food for work' programme, which cleans up entire rubbish dumps and uses the rubbish to fill in eroded parts of the roads.

Latrines are built on school yards and other public places, and activists launch public information campaigns about vaccination and other health issues.

And last but not least, activists are people who can spread the work beyond the boundaries of Sambizanga. For example, the cholera programme is active in five other areas, including the village of Caop outside town; and the support programme for EPAL, the municipal water authority is active in four other areas, including Prenda, a downtown district of flats built around 1980.

An impressive list of projects, is described more thoroughly in the booklet: *Angola, Building for the future, despite the world's worst war* (One World Action, London, 1994).

Community action

Of the Ricardo family, Rui and Zeca are long time activists, being among the first group in 1989. Altogether, the group of activists in the area consists of 65 persons, not including the workers and apprentices of the workshops, the members of the theatre group, the water monitors, the large group of inhabitants of the area (mainly women) who are active in digging for water pipelines, the refugees who work in the 'food for work' programme and so on. The whole organisation is interrelated on a personal basis: activists become workers and conversely, activists become monitors, and activists spread to other areas of town.

Rui Ricardo

"No one here in my yard suffers from a lack of food. We aren't rich, sometimes we only eat fuba and beans, but if someone has a real problem we share. But this works only for the people here in the yard, not with other neighbours, unless they're family. Normally, people here don't visit the neighbours very often - we're busy all day! So most of the people don't even know whether their neighbours are in need. Since I entered the Sambizanga Project as an activista, and started making house-to-house visits, I've got a better knowledge of the problems here in the musseque.
Because I did a good job as a volunteer, Dona Orquidea, who is the manager of the Sambizanga Project here in Ngola Kiluanje, asked me to come to work for the Local Initiatives Fund when Lucia, who had the job, began studying to become a nurse."

Zeca Ricardo

"I stopped studying when I was 22, because after the ninth class (secondary school) you need money to continue with your studies. At least you've got to go to downtown Luanda because there is no possibility for further schooling in the musseques.
When I was in the seventh grade (first class of secondary school) I started teaching, just like Rui does - that was in 1991 - and soon after a colleague of mine advised me to talk with the Sambizanga Project and I became an activista. For two years I combined studying, teaching and working for the project. I worked for the project in the morning, taught in the afternoon and went to school from 6:00 to 11:00 p.m.
As teachers, we earned 14,000 Kwanzas. You could buy a good shirt for that money, or a pair of trousers, or shoes. So it was worth something, at least. But the cost of living got higher and higher so we asked for a salary rise, which we didn't get from the government. Many teachers began to quit because it was impossible to live on the salary. I did the same and started to work as a full time activista, and in 1994 I became the manager of the *Programa de*

aterro de lixo, the 'food for work' project that is involved in cleaning up unofficial rubbish dumps. So now I also earn a salary from the project, and, fortunately, we are also paid in food, which has more value than the Kwanzas I earn."

Rubbish and roads

Zeca leads a group of refugees, mainly from the northern provinces, who started the enormous task of cleaning up the many rubbish heaps that lie scattered all over the neighbourhood. Nobody knows how long the job will last, but it will take a few years, at least, before the area will have a normal appearance again, and rubbish will be collected at better organised sites.

The group consists of 74 refugees who live in small houses - either their own, rented or with family - in the areas of Kikolo and Cimangola. They are paid with food: one kilo of food for every hour they work, generally 35 a week. Work starts at eight in the morning, when people are picked up by the lorry near their home, and they work until three in the afternoon. The group is split into six gangs, with Domingos Tunga as one of their foremen. Each gang starts

loading rubbish, which is already composted to earth in most cases, from one of the big dumps in the area. One of the three tractors of the project brings it to a road that has been prepared for it. Sometimes the potholes are more than a metre deep. After a week, usually on Fridays, a big Sambizanga Project truck brings in fresh red earth from outside the city and covers the whole road with it again. The earth is tamped down by the workers and the passing traffic. This way, more than five kilometres of roads have been repaired and seven big refuse dumps have been cleaned away. The group is now working on its third road.

Zeca signals a problem they meet nowadays: ELISAL, the municipal rubbish removal authority, does not function, at least not in the *musseques*. If these municipal services function at all, they only do so in downtown Luanda. People in the *musseques* are left to find their own solutions. Of course, this leads to renewed dumping of refuse on the newly cleaned sites. One possible solution would be for the project to build concrete containers as official rubbish collecting places, which would be serviced by ELISAL. Zeca is negotiating this matter with the vice administrator (deputy mayor) of the Municipality of Sambizanga, Mr Napoleão. Zeca's position is that the project group should be incorporated into the municipal service or, at least, given some official status so that renewed use of cleared sites can be prevented.

Friends of the environment

Amigos do meio Ambiente was founded in 1990 when a group of activists started with clean-up campaigns, tree planting campaigns and holiday events for school children. (The girls' football team is one of the successful activities of the group.) They worked with local churches and schools, but also participated in the house-to-house visits around the health centre, as described above. In these weekly visits, they cover a part of the area and inform people about the benefits of vaccinations, latrines, clearing away rubbish, treatment of water, the health centre, good mother and child care and so forth. They also hold information campaigns in schools and the health centre. There are 70 members in the group. Zeca is secretary and the rest of the board is formed by Domingos Pascoal, who organises many events, such as the football club, for children; Eduardo Colaço, who also works for the latrine project; Joaquin Baptista, who is the foreman of the small workshop in Vale Saroco; and Ottavio Maianga, who works on many projects with schools. Manuela Teka is the vice chairperson and Maria van Dunem the vice secretary.

The activistas earn food from the project, according to the amount of hours they worked. Their working hours are checked scrupulously by Dona Orquidea. Project mobilisers are full time employees and earn a basic wage as well as food.

This year, the main focus on their action is a renewed tree planting campaign. Many activities that started as limited actions have been professionalised to some extent (the health campaign is now reformed into a cholera campaign and the clean-up actions are now the 'food for work' programme). This tree project is also worthy of more attention. Many of the previously planted trees dried out and some people even used them as firewood because they are not used to keeping trees alive. For this a real campaign is needed to teach people that they need trees for a healthy environment and that they mean something for their future.

Zeca has seen many improvements since the group started five years ago. Then there was nothing, people had big heaps of rubbish in their yards, did not cover their water and answered nature's call on the streets or in their own yard. Now, hygiene conditions have improved greatly, by spreading information and by the latrine project. There are 20 water standpipes now, each with its own water 'monitor', one neighbour responsible for a particular standpipe.

This is not to say that all the problems have been solved yet. The standpipes have water only three times a week, and sometimes there is no water at all for a whole month, so people are still highly dependent on the water vendors.

Aldina Jacinto

"I work as an activista. We promote hygiene, especially for mothers and children. We hold meetings and distribute information about family planning, breast feeding, mother care, AIDS and so on. Every Friday, we make house-to-house visits, and we distribute chlorine for water treatment and ORS (oral rehydration solution) for the treatment of diarrhoea. We also accompany people to the health centre if we find them very ill. We also promote the dry pit latrine, the treatment of stagnant water and the burial of rubbish.

In the beginning, people didn't really understand what we were doing, first they took us for Jehovah's Witnesses, or for thieves, thinking that the women spied during the day and the men broke in during the night! During the political campaigns in 1992 they even took us for political campaigners! It was after we started to use the radio (LAC - Luanda Antenna Commercial) as a means of explaining what we were doing, that people eventually understood that we work with the health centre."

Unhealthy water

Because there is not enough water pumped into the municipal water system, most people buy water from vendors, whose tanks are filled with untreated river water by lorries coming from the Bengo River. Sanitation is poor. Some households have overflowing flush latrines which, together with the collected rubbish on unofficial dumps, form a very serious public health hazard.

Many people die from malaria, measles, diarrhoea, tetanus and cholera. In 1994, 262,000 cases of malaria were reported in Luanda alone, causing 19 per cent of the registered deaths that year. There were 90,000 cases of diarrhoea, 50,000 of acute respiratory diseases, 2,000 of measles. Over 20,000 deaths were recorded during 1994, 55 per cent of them children under five. The most common causes were the diseases mentioned, combined with low birth weights and malnutrition. The infant mortality rate was 160 per 1,000 - almost two in every 10 newborn babies died.

Most causes of diseases and death are related to the environment, poor water quality and sanitation, or are preventable by immunisation. These were the main reasons for making the supply of safe water one of the focal points of the Sambizanga Project.

"The municipal water system provides the city with 200,000 cubic metres per day through two water systems built by the Portuguese. From 1990 onward it was clear that this would never be enough to provide the whole population with drinking water, so one day the Baixa - downtown Luanda - would be provided, and the next day all the *musseques*", Inacio Neto, spokesperson for EPAL, the municipal water authority, told us in an interview. "This doesn't mean that everyone in the *musseques* gets water", he adds, "in fact, the pumping capacity is limited to 100,000 cubic metres per day due to maintenance problems - there are a great many leakages in the system, illegal connections and broken pipelines; and we don't have the necessary means to service it, so we are glad if we can provide people a few times a week". In Ngola Kiluanje this means that, although there is a pipeline from the main water pipe into the neighbourhood, 80 per cent of the inhabitants still depend on buying water from the vendors, who are in turn supplied by lorries who get their water from the Bengo River.

Several investigations, conducted mainly by the activists in their house-to-house visits since 1989 in Ngola Kiluanje, indicate that clean water is one of the main concerns of the neighbourhood. This information was presented to the World Bank in a report covering the whole of Luanda's *musseques*, by some of the same activists and managed by the Development Workshop support group. An additional fact that keeps a clean water supply a priority for residents of Ngola Kiluanje is that diarrhoea-related death rates are 24 times higher in the *musseques* than in downtown Luanda.

Meanwhile, three strategies have been adopted to counter the damage done by unhealthy water: first, the chlorination of river water; secondly, the repair and maintenance of standpipes in the area; and thirdly, the reproduction of the methods implemented in Ngola Kiluanje over the whole city.

Domingos de Carvalho, Ministry of Health

"After the war started again in 1992, hundreds of thousands of people fled to the city. Angolans don't like camps, so most of them stay with their families in the *musseques*, also here, in Ngola Kiluanje. And there was already an enormous shortage of water! People have to buy their water from the vendors, supplied by the lorry drivers. This water was untreated, straight from the river. I work for the Ministry of Health branch for Luanda, so we saw the danger: at first we supplied our *activistas* with chlorine to treat people's water tanks, but this clearly wasn't enough. We still had hundreds of cases of cholera here in the wet season. Now we get the help of Médecins sans Frontières and the authorities to chlorinate every tanker with water entering the city. *Activistas* only check people's tanks now and then with a 'pool tester' to see if their water still contains chlorine."

Andrew Kirkwood, Development Workshop

"We promote the installation of more standpipes with water monitors, who control them, in order to make water cheaper. Simply because people spend so much money on water nowadays it harms their capacity to buy enough food for the family. Our investigation has established that water prices vary from district to district. In Val Saroco people pay an average of UK£6 for a cubic metre of water. In *musseques* further away from the Bengo River this can be as much as UK£10! We also found that even in the immediate surroundings people paid far less if the water came from the pipeline instead of from the truck.

Meanwhile, we have to accept the fact that, in the near future, no big changes in water supply will occur, unless the pipelines can be brought back to full capacity or can be boosted by a new pipeline. For the time being, we support measures such as providing the most underprivileged areas, where the water is most expensive, with water from the system. That could be done by building pumping stations, so that the water lorries can fill up near the district, instead of driving 30 km to Kifangondo, thus saving a lot of transportation costs and reducing the prices. This will almost immediately lead to more use of water by the affected population, and leave them more money to buy food. This way, it will considerably help their standard of living and their health situation."

Water monitors

Sadi dos Santos is 35 years old. He has been monitor of Standpipe Number 4 since 1980. The standpipe did not function for a long time until it was repaired by Development Workshop May 1994. In the beginning, there was water every day, but last year only for three days a week and during the month of August 1995 not a single drop of water came out of the standpipe. "In earlier days, there was no lack of water at all; but nowadays you're never sure whether water will come to the standpipe or not. Water pressure is very low because of the many illegal connections. But neither EPAL, nor the municipal authorities, do anything about it - they lack power. Now we depend on the water from the tanks, which we have to buy for 500 Kwanzas a 20 litre bucket. People who are part of the group around the standpipe pay 200 Kwanzas a month, just for the repair fund of the standpipe. We founded a committee of four neighbours, one man, and three women. Most men consider this women's work, and it doesn't pay to be in the committee."

Domingas da Cunha, a young woman of 18, monitors the standpipe next to the health centre: "I want to be a nurse later, and I know that cleaning the standpipe can save people a lot of problems with their health. We have a committee of four people: an elderly lady of 60, one of 45 and us: a boy, Romero Lunda, and me. It's the young ones who do the work of cleaning the standpipe. We would like to invite more older people to participate for the well being of the neighbourhood!"

Local Initiatives Fund

Rui Ricardo manages an important new development for the area: the Local Initiatives Fund, which has donors from Canada and the European Union. This fund was started because the consultants of Development Workshop were aware of the many small initiatives brought forward by inhabitants of the area, varying from establishing football clubs to building classrooms. Many of these initiatives did not survive, not because of a lack of enthusiasm but simply because of a lack of money. They decided to apply for funds for a small scale Local Initiatives Fund and proposed the Sambizanga Project to manage it. The Local Initiatives Fund is one of the ways the neighbourhood can work to help itself.

Rui is in charge of the fund, having succeeded Lucia, who started the project. In normal circumstances, it would be the responsibility of the local government to establish funds like this, but the fund can be seen as an attempt to restore normal civil society in Angola.

A lot of people apply to the fund: parents' associations from almost every school in the area have asked for help with their plans, football clubs, associations of residents of the area that have no electricity and so on. There is a huge need for funds just to help people who have innovative plans to improve the living conditions in their neighbourhood.

Rui manages 20 projects now, which are evaluated regularly to fulfil the requirements of the donor organisations, as well as for the fund's own purposes. Perhaps in the longer term the number of projects would grow if more funds are made available.

School Nr. 423 is an example of one of these projects managed by Rui:

"I was able to provide school Nr. 423 with 150 bags of cement, 190 sheets of corrugated iron, and many pipes for the construction of the roof. Altogether, the material cost UK£1,500. You'd think a parents' committee could never collect a sum like this under their circumstances, but the committee has done a large part of the work already: they collected a lot of money from the parents, and many helped to start building the five classrooms. The walls are finished

already; it is the roofs, the plastering and the floors we are contributing. Our policy is to help the people who take the initiative
themselves: the parents do the building themselves or they pay the
masons to do it.

Think of it: the school has 2,700 pupils with only 12 classrooms,
and they're building five at the moment with our help. Each parent
paid 3,000 Kwanzas (about 50 UK pence) as a contribution, but
some could not even afford that. Now they can finish the building,
although they will ask parents for more contributions for the wood
and iron for doors and windows."

Transport problems

Rui can also give us examples of the many problems that arise
before projects can be carried out properly. Transport is one of
them:

"We had to bring the cement and roofing sheets to the school when
they arrived from abroad two weeks ago. So I hired a truck to carry
it and we met at ten o'clock in front of the warehouse where everything was stored: the warehouse was closed and the administrator
had not arrived yet. By eleven o'clock I had located the man and he
arrived, so we could start. But we had to carry the bags of cement
one by one, there was no fork-lift available. So we lost two hours
altogether. Then the loaded truck didn't start! The crew had listened
to music through a high volume speaker on the roof of the cab
while waiting and loading and this had used up all the energy of the
battery! It was half past two before we found another truck and
cables to start ours. Finally, we were on the road.

We had to pass the refinery and there we met a police patrol. The
officers wanted to 'check' all the details of the cargo: you need all
kind of papers here to transport things: invoices, destination papers
and so on. It's not even enough to prove you're the owner and
you're with the cargo. No, they want you to have papers from the
sending warehouse and from the destination! These are all regulations from years ago, but they still exist. Besides, nowadays police
live from *kandonga* too, so they're really keen to make some trouble if they see a truck loaded with so much merchandise. They hope
to find an irregularity to coax a few *gazosas* (soft drinks) out of you,

or better still some money, so that they can buy a beer or feed their family.

Anyway, an hour later we could proceed again and because we had all the papers we needed they had no chance to get a *gazosa*. Four hours late, we arrived at the school where the headmaster, several parents and teachers and a lot of children had been waiting for us for all this time.

But don't think we unloaded the truck and this was it. Oh no, now the very workers who had caused a good part of the delay demanded more pay because they were late! And, while at the warehouse, they had loaded four more bags of cement from the warehouse than the 150 we had paid for, and they wanted this cement. Normally, I don't agree with this sort of practice because I think they should be paid for the work they do and that's it. I don't want to promote theft! But someone from the school intervened and they got off with their bags of cement!"

Public transport

The state owned bus company (TCL) has no funds to provide adequate transport inside the city. In 1991 it owned 90 buses, of which 60 per cent are currently out of order because of the overload of passengers and lack of maintenance. It is very much the same story as with the electricity: no money, no spare parts. TCL received 100 secondhand North American school buses in 1995, but this is a drop in the ocean, not even enough for TCL to operate 40 per cent of its official lines through the city. Until it broke down in November 1994, the internal Luanda railway line handled 20 per cent of passenger transport.

This combination of official transport shortages led to the boom in *kandongeiros*. They are a form of private collective taxi, sometimes carrying up to 30 passengers packed in an old Toyota Hiace, and charging up to ten times the official public transport fare. As in the market, prices are set by the private sector.

Given that the average state employee earns around 50,000 Kwanzas and has to spend 4,000 Kwanzas per month daily on transport, it is clear why many of them simply do not show up in their offices!

Chapter 5

Local government has no power

From what we have seen, there are many spontaneous community based improvements in Ngola Kiluanje. Often, as with the Local Initiatives Fund, a little bit of help from the Sambizanga Project is enough to spark off all kinds of initiatives. These are initiatives that, in a fully functioning society, would be expected to be undertaken by local government or public groups belonging to what in the western hemisphere is generally called 'civil society'. The problem in Angola is that local government, as well as civil society, barely exist.

People here do not expect much of local government. They have almost completely lost their faith in public authorities. This is no wonder, local authorities have not invested in the district, so it is in this respect that most problems arise: not enough schools, no water, no sewer pipes, no rubbish removal system, no health care, no electricity, no roads.

The emergence of a civil society was only possible after 1990, when the 'law of free association' was introduced. Before, people could only participate in state controlled organisations.

Zeca Ricardo
"At the moment, local government has no power at all. The Commissioner has been in charge for more than 10 years now, and there has never been an election. He has the residents' committee of ten people; one for every sector, but they haven't been elected either.
At the municipal level it is a little bit better, Sambizanga, especially, has a singular place in the hierarchy because the President was born there.
But on all levels, it would be better if there were elections. The good

people would stay in power, being re-elected, and the bad ones would simply disappear. It's also important for the commune. If you have someone who 'has a voice' and uses it, who fights for his constituency, more will happen because of it."

Historical background

After independence, Angola inherited a centrally controlled government structure from the Portuguese. This repressive centralising tendency was reinforced by Portugal's own long fascist regime, which was not overthrown until 1974. The modernisation of Portugal continues still.

To add to this, the MPLA, the party that won the war of independence in 1975, adopted a Marxist-Leninist model of central planning in which the Ministry of Planning is the country's superpower. This is hardly the way to reverse the top-down structure established by colonialism.

The Angolan economy, in which most revenue is earned from petroleum sales and all taxes are derived from exporting oil and diamonds or importing goods, tends to accentuate this structure. There has never been a way of taxing or raising public funds locally, only

from these exports and imports. Every project, or even annual budget spending on maintaining services, is approved by the Ministry of Planning and Economy, which also holds the funds. This imposes a rigid planning cycle, in which there is no room for new initiatives, not even for funds to counter emergencies.

This was the situation prior to the peace agreement in 1991 and it continues today, despite new legislation to the contrary. Following the agreement, new legislation was passed to ensure multiparty democracy and national elections. But the legal changes for elections have not succeeded in reaching the provincial, municipal and communal levels, a situation which is also due to the resumption of war in 1992.

Luanda: in transition to the unknown

Luanda, including the municipalities of Viana and Cacuaco, is one of Angola's 18 provinces, the smallest in area but home to the largest population. Luanda's Governor is Justino Fernandez. Like all other Governors he is appointed by the President. The nine municipal administrators or 'commissioners', as people sometimes still call them, are appointed by the Governor, as are the 24 communal administrators.

Despite their high-level appointments, many of these officials deplore the situation. They find themselves in a rigid top-down command structure in which they appear to have power, but really have little because of the lack of resources and their dependence on their political and administrative superiors. Given that the party itself is not democratically organised, it is obvious that democracy in Angola does not extend to the level of the *musseques*. In any case, with an ancient history of hierarchical African structures, 500 years of oppressive colonial rule and 20 years of rigid Marxist-Leninism, it would be surprising if democracy could be established within a few years.

This is the situation of Angolan society at the moment: everybody knows it is in transition, yet nobody knows where it going. The warring parties hold each other hostage, so that for the time being the well intentioned politicians can only stick it out, and corruption can continue to flourish, filling foreign bank accounts.

Supporting this entrenched hierarchy, is the rigid structure of the executive ministries such as health, education, social services and security, in which resources and decision making are centralised, thus undermining the executive officers of the local authorities.

The Governor

Justino Fernandez, Luanda's Governor, and as such a cabinet minister, admits his relative powerlessness to solve the numerous problems of the city. To him, the problems appear worse than he had ever imagined before he became Governor. Questioned about almost every major problem, he has to recognise that he can draw up a plan, but that the Presidency simply does not give him the means to implement it.

The reason: the war.

In the case of ELISAL, the city's rubbish removal service, he has been able to solve some problems, but only in the 'asphalt city' - downtown, by encouraging small groups of road sweepers to form their own enterprises and to try to get their funds from the city's shopkeepers and other entrepreneurs. His administration has no funds for them, so they have no trucks or other facilities, only their brooms and shovels.

The rainy season creates thousands of victims every year, not only directly by damaging roads and pavements and even houses, but also indirectly by contributing to widespread malaria, cholera and diarrhoea. In the rainy season, Luanda's streets are dotted with pools of stagnant water, a mixture of sewer water and rain.

Governor Fernandez openly complains about the Ministry of Planning and Economy, saying that in any other capital in the world the city authority receives enough money to cover its direct needs at least, except in Angola. When he started this job, he developed the 'Let's save Luanda' plan, in which the city's authorities launched an appeal to tackle many of the problems of Luanda (water supply, rains, roads, sanitation, rubbish dumps, transport, building and health problems like cholera and malaria). Cost: UK£200 million. Result: no money allocated 'due to the war'.

Still, he seems to do what he can, encouraging the building of standpipes for the supply of water all over the city instead of only repairing the pipes feeding the houses in downtown Luanda, and defend-

ing this in the press. The Governor himself is hoping that after the war is really over, about 50 per cent of the influx of people of the last 10 years will return to their villages. He hopes in the long term to be able to build a city for two million people instead of the almost three million inhabiting the city at the moment. But, at the same time, he is clear that he does not expect this to happen soon.

Unplanned urbanisation

Luanda's city centre, surrounded as it is by the populous self-built *musseques*, cannot expand. A study by Filipe Colaço shows that around 14 per cent of the city is occupied by the modern centre; 26 per cent is in transition, made up of former *musseques* that have been gradually incorporated into the city by planned building of flats, for instance; and over 50 per cent is *musseques*. He calculated a shortage of at least 300,000 houses, even if at least part of the influx due to the war would return home. And, since 1987 no more housing schemes have been carried out. Worse still, there is simply no planning. In the *musseques* people build their houses wherever they can; if someone makes a request for building permission to the local government, a delay of two years can be expected before getting an answer, if an answer comes at all. Of course, in the meantime someone else builds on the same spot. So it has become common practise to construct first and apply for permission afterwards.

New plans for self-building

Justino Fernandes has publicly acknowledged the inefficiency of his provincial authority and the impossibility of restructuring the *musseques*. Therefore, he has launched a plan called 'Luanda Sul', a programme to build new housing districts in the south of Luanda, creating an urban area of 57 square kilometres, providing housing for 200,000 people by 1999.

By designing a new residential area, with shops, enterprises, tourist sites, parks, schools and other amenities, and selling the building sites of this area to large enterprises or individuals, he hopes to generate enough income for the project to be able to finance the design of two more areas with housing estates, including the necessary infrastructure: water from the Kwanza River in the south and access roads from downtown Luanda.

Fernandes is advised in this matter by the Brazilian multinational,

Odebrecht, which apparently understands that this kind of planning has nothing to expect from government budgets and has to be self-financed. They maintain that this kind of project does not need foreign capital. But others, especially NGOs, hold serious doubts that these goals can be reached with the limited resources the provincial government has at its disposal.

The Communal Commissioner

Antonio Sebastião is last in the hierarchy of the local authorities. He is Commissioner of the Commune of Ngola Kiluanje, one of three communes of the Municipality of Sambizanga. His office is on the main road of Ngola Kiluanje. It lacks any kind of facility you would expect of an office, and could use a coat of paint. Folders are stacked on the floor because there is no money for filing cabinets; he has one administrative clerk in the office, but no money for a typewriter. Nevertheless, he is the Mayor and Chief of Police of a community of at least 80,000 people, of which an estimated 20,000 entered the area after 1992. His commune covers nine square kilometres and contains many enterprises of which the national refinery and the Roque Santeiro market are the largest.

Mr. Sebastião has a clear vision of the problems of the *musseque* and of his own limitations. He is especially unhappy that many people in the area see him as a puppet of the government. He hopes to be able to prove this is not so, once he achieves financial autonomy, officially given to the communes by law in 1992 but still not implemented. "We have the refinery in our area, and many other big enterprises, and yet they do not allow us to tax them", he says in an interview, "and if we have to write a letter we have to borrow a typewriter, and beg for paper!" He sees very well the need for municipal independence: "Once the law for local finance is approved, we can work on democracy here", he adds; "at the moment, we can sit together with anyone we want and no one is going to supply us with the necessary money."

Mr. Sany, one of the concerned employers in the district, agrees:
"In this respect, it would not be bad at all if some neighbourhood
or youth organisation would organise themselves again, as in earlier days. We would be most happy to help them. If you see how few
opportunities the administration of the commune has; everything
is centralised. They are no more than decoration and have no power
at all. We need more decentralisation; it doesn't function the way
it is now. We cannot work on the most important problems the area
faces, like the streets that deteriorate year after year - not even
repairs are carried out after the rains."

Development of the *musseques* is severely hindered by the chron-
ic weakness of public administration. Luanda suffers more from
these problems than any other province and the presence of the central government continually causes confusion. In the first place,
the cleverer Luanda functionaries are quickly drawn into the national system, leaving the city with the rest. Secondly, the direct interventions of the higher levels of political power, meddle in the area
of provincial or municipal authorities. This deprives these administrators of the little authority they have and causes their alien-
ation from the system, leading to obstruction and a lack of cooperation. In their turn, public officials often tend to an undemocratic
abuse of power at their own level of bureaucracy.

Teresa Correia Gomez

Teresa Correia Gomez works for the water programme: "I'm a social
mobiliser. It is my job to organise people around the standpipes in
committees to assure they themselves take the responsibility for
maintenance and cleaning and that they continue to do so in the
long run. Recently, we started working in several new districts.
There we try to find out whether the old structures of people's
organisation still exist. Sometimes we find that people have already
organised themselves, in their blocks or buildings, around rubbish
removal, sewer pipes or security issues.
In my own area, Terra Nova, a new district of Rangel municipality,

there are no existing structures. In Rangel itself, the so-called demo-cratic 'residents committee' is full of municipal functionaries, and there have never been elections. So it can happen, that in fact the role of these committees is repressive, not active. I know of a case where the administration made it impossible for people to travel outside Luanda (until recently, Angolans needed a *guia de marcha*, a travel permit, for internal journeys) because they refused to coop-erate with the 'residents committee'. Fortunately, we also meet resi-dents' committees and local commissioners who really work for the well being of their area and make efforts to convince people, instead of bullying them.

But at the moment, there are more good functioning water commit-tees, not belonging to any governmental structure, consisting of four or five volunteers, with a full time paid standpipe monitor and cleaner. Generally, they are 'elected' by a 'constituency' of 15 or 20 people who come to the regular residents' meetings and around 50 people who pay a small amount for maintenance of the standpipe."

No faith in political parties

These days, politics is also pretty much discredited in the *musseques*. Many people have come to see the MPLA as a repressive party, rather than a solution to their problems. At the same time, they feel themselves to be a part of the MPLA because of their shared history, so they find it difficult to commit themselves to another party, especially if these parties start to establish the same non-democratic internal party practices.

Nevertheless, during the 'short peace' and the elections of 1992, many parties - but mainly the MPLA and UNITA - campaigned openly and freely in Ngola Kiluanje. Most other parties had very few supporters in the *musseque* and they only rallied downtown. For the elections, UNITA invaded the area with banners and posters and small campaigning offices based in people's homes. From motorcycles, they handed out trinkets to youngsters who campaigned for them, and they even had armed soldiers behaving like a parallel police. Quite a few people, especially from the provinces where UNITA traditionally has a broad base, but also youngsters who saw a career before them, wore UNITA tee-shirts (not least because they owned few or no other clothes) and hung posters in front of their houses. Accepting this was not easy for the vast MPLA majority living in the area, but there were no attacks; a few (mainly drunken) skirmishes, a bit of shouting against the other parties, but no real threat to the fragile peace process. On the contrary, there was a movement towards bipolarisation in an area that had been a 'one-party state' for over 20 years.

The election in September 1992 was the pinnacle of this political evolution. In general, the process can be seen as a sincere display of the goodwill of the people of the area that they too were tired of the war and willing to prove that disputes could be settled in a peaceful way. The hours that so many people, of different parties, waited in line to cast their vote was convincing enough.

Unfortunately, the resumption of the war in 1992 and the horrors of the fighting in Luanda itself put an end to this labouriously constructed goodwill.

Rui Ricardo

"I will never belong to a political party, nor will I get myself involved in politics. Of course I feel MPLA, because of my background, but I would never want to support them publicly or discuss politics like other hotheads do. Not for the MPLA, not for UNITA. Of course I would go to vote if there are elections - voting is free isn't it! But politics here in the district? Look, the district is large and has many problems, so who knows, some things could be solved with the same dedication as a political party - like the Sambizanga Project is doing for the neighbourhood. Other institutions, even a political party or a local NGO, or an association, could help.

The real problem is that almost no one here is mature and independent enough to defend the neighbourhood; to fight for this district; to discuss the problems of the epidemics, the rubbish, the energy, the water, and all the others. Maybe even a political party could be of advantage for the community. But that ought to be in cooperation with the community and at the moment not even the MPLA has a structure in the area. They only have the commissioner, and that man has absolutely no power.

Still, people are talking of a change in leadership here in the district. Maybe if there would be elections people would prefer to vote for someone who has more financial power, like Mr. Sany. He established a bakery, a shop and a disco; and he erected street lamps. He is willing to invest, and he is not planning to rob the community. But it is not easy to organise people here. Many people just aren't trustworthy. We have had no electricity for two years now, as you know. A year ago, a self-appointed 'residents committee' collected 1,000 Kwanzas from all the households to pay EDEL for a new transformer. Nobody knows where the money went, but everybody knows there still ain't no electricity!"

Electrical overload

The many problems in delivering electricity to Luanda have their origins in the poor state of the Hydroelectric Cambambe Electricity Station, 180 km from Luanda, and the main power line between the station and Luanda. Rationing and interruptions of delivery are generally caused by problems in one of the four generators or in the high tension line.

José Marinho, director of the National Electricity Board: "The main problem is the maintenance of the high tension pylons. First of all, this line is a favourite sabotage target for UNITA. Innumerable times pylons have been blown up and repaired temporarily under difficult military circumstances. On top of this, the military have decided to prevent sabotage like this by placing land mines in the surrounding fields. These mines prevent us from maintaining the lines! So we started to defuse our own mines, but this is a long term process which came to a halt with the resumption of the war in 1992. Furthermore, the four generators in the dam have not been replaced in 30 years, causing regular breakdowns."

EDEL, the municipal electricity authority, has no stocks for maintaining lines or transformers. According to Nsiansoki Mayamoni, technical director of EDEL: "We need at least one and a half million dollars a year for maintenance parts to assure our clients the minimal necessary service. But we never get this money from the Ministry of

Planning and Economy, so we're not able to import enough stocks. We have to repair damaged items in a provisional way, knowing that within months or even days the same thing will break down again. Nevertheless, we have been able, with Swedish and Spanish help, to repair a major part of the distribution network and three substations in the city. For the *musseques* the future is still unknown. Transformers burn out through the heavy overcharge caused by illegal connections. We cannot control them simply because they are illegal and people hide the connections as well as they can!

In the Bairo dos Ossos and the Kwanzas Market this is the case indeed, but we are working on it now: we are investigating a number of consumers at present and will replace the burnt transformer afterwards. At the moment, Ngola Kiluanje is not the only place where we cannot deliver electricity. It is the same in Palanca, Golfe, Cazenga and Rocha Pinto. The problem is that we have no transformers; and if we simply replace a burnt one with a new one, it will burn out within months because of the overload."

The backbone of the new civil society

Although most 'old' organisational structures, such as 'residents committees' are discredited or dysfunctional, there is indeed a boom in emerging associations, community based organisations and NGOs, made possible by the liberalisation of Angolan society that began in 1990.

One reason for this apparent boom is that many churches are now registering associations that existed long before 1990. Such church related organisations have provided health and educational facilities in the *musseques* for a number of years, and have so far been able to improve services considerably. Many Angolan NGOs evolved from within the security provided by these churches.

FONGA (Forum of Angolan Nongovernmental Organisations) was formed in 1991 to provide an opportunity for NGOs to communicate and cooperate with each other. FONGA has a membership ranging from very professional, well established, organisations such as ADRA (Action for the Development of Rural Angola and the Environment), AALSIDA (the Angolan AIDS committee), AIA (protestant churches) AAD (Angolan Action for Development), to very small organisations, which, for example, might run only one small health post somewhere in the *musseques*. Examples of these are the IEU (United Evangelican Church), the Kimbangista Church, ACM (Angolan YMCA), ACORSDR, IESPA, IESA, IMA, ACEA, and SCAN. There are many more. As the possibility is there, the number of grassroots people's organisations, also in the *musseques,* is steadily growing. It must be said that many of them are still fragile; they have no staff - only volunteers, they have no funds - sometimes a few dollars from abroad, and they have no experience - but a lot of good will to start improving life in their immediate surroundings. This, in itself, is an important issue: foreign NGOs could identify the most promising of these organisations and help them to form the backbone of the new civil society that Angola so desperately needs.

Development Workshop

Mary Daly, one of Development Workshop's directors, explains: "It is very important to strengthen these local structures. After all, these are the people who will build up a new civil society of emancipated people, who will not let themselves be easily oppressed, and it is this Angola needs most. After all, the inherited colonial system has never really been transformed. What we need is a pluralist, participatory democracy, not just another party taking over from the MPLA. Look, for instance, to the strike of the teachers, who are really challenging the system to pay them at least salaries on which they can survive and dedicate themselves to teaching, instead of corruption or small scale trade. The war has long been a pretext to go on in the old way, but more and more people refuse to take that for granted.

We can only hope that people will look at other parties, in the first place UNITA, with the same eyes. As one politician said here: 'we don't need stereo-partyism instead of mono-partyism. We don't need the same music while we only hear the instruments better!'

From our practice in the Sambizanga Project we see that it takes years before people start organising themselves around concrete themes like water. It takes a lot of time to build up enough self-esteem to organise yourself around your own needs. We see a good combination in developing basic needs together with social and cultural needs: people will learn by doing. We have seen activistas developing themselves as responsible people, worthy to work for their fellow inhabitants. These might be the people we'll hear from in the future, but the whole process will take a long, long time."

Chapter 6

The war and its impact
on life in Luanda

For most inhabitants of Ngola Kiluanje, the fighting in Luanda - 31st of October until the 2nd of November 1992 - was their main direct confrontation with warfare. It had been happy days around the time of the elections of 29th and 30th of September, and many people still recall the rows of people quietly standing in line to cast their votes, regardless of their political affiliation. But soon after the elections, UNITA started to complain about irregularities and fraud, especially when a quick count by the United Nations had resulted in the expectation that UNITA would loose. On the 5th of October, UNITA withdrew its officers from the combined army (the FAA), a clear signal of things to come.

The U.N. Security Council, concerned about the situation, dispatched a commission from Cape Verde, Morocco, Russia and the United States to investigate the allegations while the results of the elections were kept unpublished. On the 17th of October, the National Electoral Council announced the official results after the U.N. committee had declared that in none of the 18 Angolan provinces had evidence been found of electoral fraud. In the legislative elections the MPLA had won 53 per cent of the votes, UNITA 34 per cent.. For the presidency, Dos Santos (MPLA) had won 49.5 per cent, Savimbi (UNITA) 40 per cent. This meant another round of elections between these two candidates, because more than 50 per cent was necessary to win without a second election. This election for the presidency has never been held.

It was UNITA who launched a nationwide operation to occupy municipalities and towns, killing administrators and election authorities at random. On the 31st of October, fighting broke out in Luanda, resulting in the evacuation of foreigners and many casualties among the inhabitants of the city. After three days came a victory by the MPLA, thanks mainly to the civilian population who had been armed by the police and other government authorities, and who took an active part in the fighting. Especially along the main road in Ngola Kiluanje, many retreating UNITA soldiers were killed by MPLA soldiers, civilians, police and units of the riot police. People still do not like to talk about the horror of what they call the *confusão*.

Meanwhile, quiet has returned to the city, but wounds have not healed. Many UNITA supporters were killed, as well as many from the MPLA side, and many UNITA supporters fled, some of whom are still with UNITA in the countryside, while others returned at the beginning of 1993, now living in relative peace with their neighbours again.

Still living with the *confusão*

The polarisation caused by the events of 1992 was disastrous for democracy. Most of the people learned that political parties cannot be trusted and that politicians do not bother about the *musseques*, except if they want to win votes and that, if you campaign for them, you can be killed for it. Furthermore, they learned that you cannot trust your neighbours, they might be secret supporters of the other party, or they might even kill you in another *confusão*, if they find you belong to the 'wrong' party. So most people lick their wounds inside their homes and just try to survive.

It is no wonder then that when many people start assuring you that they are non-political, they do not necessarily mean that they have no programme for the area or that they do not sympathise with any of the political parties. Most often, it means that they do not want to be associated with the warrior parties, that they are peaceful citizens, waiting for the time to come when the bipolarisation is over and they can start talking about issues again instead of 'politics', which to them means only quarrelling and fighting. Reconciliation in Luanda has become very difficult, especially after the disaster of 1992.

Half a million people have died directly from warfare since the end of 1992. Another half a million died through preventable diseases and famine caused by the war. In 1993, the United Nations Secretary General, Boutros Boutros Ghali, declared the war in Angola "the worst in the world". Nevertheless, the estimated 10 million land mines (one for every Angolan citizen) cause deaths daily, even though most of the fighting ceased in November 1994. The enormous damage around Luanda, and other cities like Huambo, Kuito and Malanje, and throughout the whole countryside, indirectly creates victims every day through malnutrition, related diseases and general lack of health care.

Every day, life in Luanda continues to be prejudiced by the war, merely by the fact that 60 per cent of the population did not come here out of their own free will, but as refugees. This is compounded by the additional facts that they are barely able to stay afloat financially and that many have lost several family members over the past 30 years.

Furthermore, the resumption of the war in 1992 was accompanied by fierce fighting in Luanda, and in Ngola Kiluanje. People still recall the horrendous images of those days. And the war is not really over. Freedom of movement inside the country has not been restored, causing enormous problems for the market traders of Luanda, resulting in high prices, more inflation, and enormous stress and strain for everyone.

Victims of the war

Many women lost their source of family income from the formal economy when their husbands died in military service, or when family members died in the *confusão* of 1992.

Many orphans live on the streets, trying to make a living selling newspapers or whatever they are able to get hold of.

Many others have become victims to the cholera epidemics. In total, an estimated 250,000 people, in Luanda alone, live in circumstances of the most extreme poverty.

In Bungo, at a crossroads near the main road to Ngola Kiluanje, in a big hole caused by the rainwater flowing away from the roads, three buildings have been erected. Two are made out of cardboard, and the other is built more solidly using the carcass of an old car. Together, 75 people live in these shacks: refugees from outside Luanda, demobilised soldiers and street children. Thirty of them are between six and 15 years old. Manuel Calaboca, not much more than 1.5 metres tall and nicknamed 'Manecas', is the natural leader of this community: Manecas was a soldier in the government army, but got wounded in 1992 in Huambo, in one of the fiercest battles. He was transported back to the coast when his convoy was hit by an ambush: the car he was in struck a mine and UNITA soldiers opened fire. The ambush later became known as the 'Kipungo massacre'. He still does not know who saved him and took him to a hospital in Luanda where, three days later, he regained consciousness. He had a broken leg, a broken jaw and his throat had a severe wound. But there was no one to care for him in the hospital and after his wounds had more or less healed, he was thrown out because no one was there to pay for him. He tried to get money to return to Lubango, the city where his family lived, but he could not get enough for the fare. No military or civil authority was willing to help him, claiming they bore no responsibility for him.

Now he lives, still half sick, among these shacks, built by himself and the many friends he has made wandering around the streets of Luanda. Most of them are ex-soldiers. Together, they house the street children, and they try to make a living begging and selling together. The one that brings in the most money is a wounded ex-soldier with a drain still attached to his stomach. He, too, was sent away from hospital because of a lack of money. Fortunately, people pity him and he can share his income with others. The man who lost both legs in a minefield, and now pushes himself around on a pallet with wheels, also brings in a lot of money. Fortunately, they have been helped a lot by the staff of an hotel, who give them food regularly.

This is only one of the thousands of stories people can tell you. Some may sound extreme and exaggerated, but a great deal of their evidence has been confirmed. Indeed, people without money are not accepted in hospitals or are thrown out before they have recovered. Many soldiers who were wounded in similar circumstances are reported to have been demobilised, and thus no longer the responsibility of the military. The Red Cross orthopaedic centre in Viana confirms that many soldiers who lost their legs prefer to beg without prostheses because they make more money that way.

Pai, Ricardo Vieira

"I was born in 1938 in Pango, a village in Bengo province. I learned the trade of a carpenter, earning my living until I served in the Portuguese colonial army in Goa, India, from 1956 to 1958. By the time I got back, my father had died and I had inherited a part of the land he owned - a forest, in fact, because my brothers had taken the best parts of the inheritance as they were there when he died. I married Teresa in 1958, and we started to work the land: bit by bit, we cleared the land and planted coffee. The Portuguese landowners for whom I worked as a carpenter paid me with the labour of their workforce, not in money. We had quite a large farm at the end! Fernando, my oldest son, was born there and later the rest of the children - all of them were born there. From 1961, the war against the Portuguese started. There was a lot of fighting in the neighbourhood. The MPLA and FNLA attacked the Portuguese, but we managed to stay there.

The real problems began after 1975, when UNITA arrived on the scene. They attacked everyone, accusing them of working with the government: they destroyed all the houses in the neighbourhood, but not mine: I later heard that it was nice enough for a UNITA commander to live in. We had fled to the city in 1978, so we survived, but once the war is over, I would prefer to go back there - we own that place! If my children will help me, I will return and live in peace again as a farmer.

It's the war that makes life expensive here. UNITA burns the cars and convoys that come out of the province to provide the city with food. This way, no vegetables enter Luanda, and so prices are too high for the scarce goods sold at the markets. In times of peace we would live better because Angola is full of food; we have the seeds and everything grows here! As far as I'm concerned, this war may stop today; I most certainly don't want it!

Apart from the difficulties of life every Angolan has the tragedy of at least one victim: Fernando, my son, was a pilot in the airforce. In 1983 we got the message that he had disappeared with his plane. His colleagues thought he defected to UNITA, to Jamba, but we never got a message from him. One day he was heard on UNITA's radio Vorgan, but after that nobody ever heard from him. Nobody knows what happened. In 1991, with the first peace we expected him to show up, but he never came."

Adão Cumandala

"Before 1992 I was a Major in the army, I commanded a battalion of tanks, four groups each of four tanks. But I didn't aspire to be a Colonel or a General - that's nice in peacetime but not in war. In fact, I had enough of war, being in the army for 14 years. I was born in 1963 and my generation has never had a happy childhood: our youth was marked by the war. I have no memories of happy events in my adolescence, only of war. And after all these years of fighting, when the possibility came in 1992 to demobilise, I decided it had been enough for me. I wanted to contribute to my country in another way. I hoped to specialise in civil construction, or in journalism. So I demobilised just before the elections in 1992. It was not easy to adapt to the civil society I must say, after so many years of military behaviour and being used to a certain standard of living, it was not easy at all! We had a right to a pension for six months, but we only got it once, for one month, and then nothing more. We also had the right to some training courses, but these schemes didn't work out either. I barely managed to survive. I lived with my family who helped me through. Without them I would not have known how to survive. I do have a lot of old comrades who live in very bad circumstances, not worthy of their rank in the army. They have had to do a lot of work that isn't really honest: 'organise' things, selling them etcetera.

In the time of the *confusão*, my friends and I judged that we had the moral responsibility not to stand with folded arms, but to help restore order. We formed resistance groups, with the collaboration of the city's police, there was no army at that time, the former army was demobilised and the new one, the FAA, had not yet formed combat groups. Only UNITA had not demobilised and was able to take over town after town.

I followed the situation after the elections when UNITA started to occupy villages and cities. We also found out that UNITA planned to take over certain areas of town. Lots of people decided they had to do something and they started to organise themselves. They demanded arms from the police headquarters in their neighbourhood. So, being an ex-Major, I became leader of a group in my neighbourhood, waiting for things to come. We were regularly informed by the police command that the tension was mounting. From the 20th of October, when UNITA started taking over numerous villages and cities, everybody became afraid of them taking over Luanda.

So on the 30th of October it was the police commander of my neighbourhood who informed us that there was proof that UNITA would occupy Luanda and many other cities immediately. We took counter action and prevented them taking Luanda by throwing them out of the city. Three days of fighting inside the city - now known as the *confusão* - followed. UNITA retreated mainly towards Kaxito, right through our neighbourhood. It was here where Salupeto Pena, the highest ranking UNITA official in Luanda, got killed.

After Luanda was free from UNITA, we returned home again. For us, fighting was over. It was only in May 1993 that I joined in the rebuilt FAA again.

Meanwhile, we survived by our own basic means - always in war people help each other! We simply ate with neighbours: whoever had food shared it. We had to 'organise' or buy things and sell them again. After May, I received a salary again as an artillery Major in the restructured army, and we started to move towards Kaxito. After a few months, Kaxito was liberated and later we retook Ndalatando. Others went on to Uige, Malanje, Zaire (the Angolan province, *Ed.*), but I stopped and demobilised. I wanted to live with my family again and build up a civilian life. Enough time in the army for me!"

Powerful interests at stake

Many people in Luanda believe that only a miracle will turn the ongoing peace process into a lasting peace. There are too many powerful groups that have interests in continuing the war.

Of course, there is UNITA - Jonas Savimbi and his army leaders. They control two thirds of Angolan territory and more than half the diamond mining, from which their personal wealth comes. They have not much to gain from this uncertain peace, by which their personal well being is not guaranteed. More than once, UNITA has held up the peace process in order to gain from the *status quo*. This happened several times after 1975. There are very few signs that this time UNITA would accept less than a total victory.

But the same applies to many government officials. In Angola, like many other African countries, it is almost impossible to build up personal wealth without being in power. Industry is not an alternative, as it barely functions. Trade, oil and diamond revenues are fully controlled by the state, so gaining official status provides the only opportunity for those whose main aim is the development of their personal capital.

The situation in the diamond area is a good example. As long as diamond-digging government generals do not meddle in the territory claimed by their UNITA counterparts, peace is secured. But any change in the fragile *status quo* ("These are my diamonds - hands off!") can lead to an outbreak of war in Lunda province, where the diamonds are mined.

In addition, some high ranking government officials get payoffs from import licences and currency trading in the super inflation that characterises Angola's present economy. For instance, merely by bringing Angolan currency from government territory to UNITA territory, where the exchange rate is lower, someone can earn millions of dollars.

It is not the intention of this book to describe all the possible forms of fraud in Angola, but it must be said that every day more are invented as a result of this complex and lawless situation. Unfortunately, many people in power on both sides profit from it and have no motive to bring an end to these personally advantageous conditions.

The deadly *status quo* is maintained

Intervention from abroad is very difficult, if not impossible. Nevertheless, there is a lot of intervention already, from arms traders and multinationals who sell all kinds of commodities to both parties, paid for with the revenues from oil (government) and diamonds (UNITA). The arms traders especially, whose estimated turnover for the past three years is three times the Angolan annual income from oil and diamonds - 21 billion US dollars, are not expected to help bring peace to the country.

At present, the United Nations implements the so-called United Nations Angola Verification Mission - UNAVEM III (yes indeed, this is the third programme, the war having been resumed twice), costing US$1 million a day and its effectiveness is minimal. There is a lot of international political pressure on both parties, in the first place by President Mandela of South Africa, but also by many other African, American and European heads of state. They are clear that they expect peace in Angola, but they have no means to impose it. All this makes a continuation of the *status quo* (a win-win situation, from the point of view of the warring parties) more likely than the birth of a lasting peace.

Meanwhile, it is the great majority of Angola's population that suffer the consequences. An estimated 50 per cent live in absolute poverty, near starvation, another 40 per cent survive mainly thanks to the fact they live, like the Ricardo family, in cities where 'buying and selling' is a way of life and they have access to food aid. The next eight per cent are relatively wealthy, and the top two per cent can be considered super-rich, the exploiters of all this misery. In April 1996 there was still no freedom of movement inside the country. Both warring parties control their respective territories, exploiting this situation by imposing random taxes on people who dare to cross the line. Don Redding, a senior official of Save the Children Fund (U.K.) commented on the development and relief aid pledged at the Donors Round Table in Brussels, September 1995: "Money or no money, development is not possible while the population remains divided geographically and militarily. The lack of freedom of movement poses a two-way problem of access: relief agencies [even the UN, *Ed.*] will have difficulty getting proper access to people in UNITA zones; but also, those people will have difficulty getting access to services. This problem of access also applies to economic security, ... the basic marketplace is severely distorted because of people's lack of freedom to move from one zone to

Cuidado com os fios das minas!

another to trade agricultural produce for basic consumer goods."
It is this mechanism that forms one of the main obstacles to the
development of Luanda's markets, thus bringing about many hard-
ships for the people who live in the city as well as those in the
countryside.

Ambrosio Pimentel

"For the time being I don't have much confidence in peace. The parties have been talking about it for months now, but they never stick to their word. Today they promise something and tomorrow they do something else. This peace is a paper peace, the population doesn't see anything of it.

Everything at the market is expensive. Rice, for instance, is imported, not because we do not grow it in Angola but because nobody is working the fields at the moment. Anyway, whatever is produced doesn't reach the markets. We do have fields of our own, but they're beyond reach in Piri, UNITA territory. My parents still live there, the only way of contact is by way of other people - we can't visit them. I grew up amidst the coffee fields: my father has always grown coffee. But they don't produce because of the war. If these warlords would only stop and allow us peace, we would have many sorrows less!"

Teresa Correia Gomez

"Originally I worked in Lubango, in Huila province. I did more or less the same work there, also for the national water authority. But there is a big difference between people there and here in Luanda! People here are frustrated, they work all day to earn themselves a little bit of money, or they steal or prostitute themselves. In the provinces, people have at least the possibility to live off their fields, to grow their own crops. Here people almost cannot work as volunteers, they're always slaving, they're mad with sorrow.

Neither will you find a traditional system of organisation, of the African life, here in town. But it still exists in the provinces. There you find whole traditional families living in the same yard: grandparents, children, grandchildren, men with more wives living in huts near to each other. That is very seldom seen here. Indeed, men have kept their attitude to polygamy, but now they have more women who live in different small houses, and the men take care of none of them! Old headmen, Sobas, are still an important factor in the province: they pass on old customs, they educate the people and they teach them how to respect each other. You won't find them here in town. Nowadays, you may find schooling in Luanda, but there is far less education: people are uprooted, they have left their traditional values in the provinces they came from, all the provinces, and all kinds of different values. And now they have to live with all these different cultures here in town, with too many people and yet nothing has come in the place of their old values. The war has brought a lot of material damage, but maybe this moral and social damage is even worse, and will take more time even to restore.

The big difference between the big city of Luanda and the country-side is the people's behaviour, the war has caused an enormous moral decay. Not only for the soldiers who learned nothing but slaughtering, but also for the common people, most of whom are very frustrated. They do not have the even minimal conditions to live a human life. In the countryside, people can at least grow their own crop, and everything is cheaper, certainly basic food products. Here, just to survive, people do all kinds of weird things. They steal, they do all kinds of lousy work and they try to make profits over other people's heads, even of their friends. And all this because of the high costs of living.

I would really like to see education and development to go hand in hand here, but this is very long term work, especially as far as public spirit is concerned this will take a long time in this ruin of a country."

Chapter 7

From nightmares of the past
to dreams for the future

To an outsider, Angola probably looks like a peculiar combination of Kuwait (oil dollars) and Haiti (poorest country in the world), whose problems are compounded by a pointless war and widespread corruption.

To the Luandan women in the market and men in the street, these unappealing features of a nation in crisis are the ever-present backdrop to the reality of daily life. Women, especially, have to deal with economic survival by generating most of their income in the informal economy (Chapter 3). This means that economic development cannot take place without including gender as a key point of analysis and without acknowledging the central and leading role played by women in the economy.

Building a place in which to live and develop is a 'do-it-yourself' activity in Luanda (Chapter 4), where there is no local government with enough power to provide people with the basic services they might normally expect (Chapter 5). So far, people have responded to this problem by starting to organise themselves, however slowly, in community based organisations and sometimes in non-governmental development organisations. This is a starting point from which to develop a real civil society, a society organised from the bottom up, where free people can organise themselves in ways they see as appropriate and by this, defend their own interests.

Clearly, this is a long term proposition, as Teresa Gomez says in Chapter 6. There are many obstacles to be removed before Angolan and Luandan societies can function normally.

Language is power: regional politics in Angola

One of the main obstacles to civil society is a deep discord among the Angolan peoples. Centuries of domination of the Kimbundu speaking, who live around Luanda, over the Ovimbundu speaking, who live around the central highlands of Huambo, is one of them. This ethnic split is still an important factor in UNITA maintaining a firm and strategically important base in Huambo.

Another difference is that which exists between *mestiços*, people of mixed Portuguese and African race, and the original Africans. For generations, the *mestiços* have dominated the country, first under the Portuguese, later as the intellectuals who fought the Portuguese but who again dominated the leadership of the MPLA.

There is also a big difference between the people from the town and from the countryside. 'Town' means Luanda first of all, but also the provincial capitals, tied to Luanda by an airborne network and cut off from their hinterland for decades. The towns have lived under MPLA rule for the past 20 years, while the countryside has lived under UNITA or other movements, or has had no rule at all.

David Birmingham, Professor of Modern History at the University of Kent, who has taught in many African countries including Angola, expresses this in terms of language in a speech to the Cambridge Congress, and later published in *Why Angola Matters* (1994):

"Angola has been divided for the last 100 years into the people of the city who speak Portuguese as their native mother tongue and the people of the countryside who speak various dialects of Bantu and use Portuguese as their vernacular language of wider communication. In the last 20 years these two traditions have been at war with one another. ...

One hundred years ago the great black families of the Angolan Coastal towns - with Portuguese and Dutch names such as Dos Santos and Van Dunem - called themselves proudly 'the Natives' .... Their roots lie in many cases in the army and their language was the language of army command ... It was these families who found-ed the MPLA in the fifties together with the assimilated black fam-ilies with whom they shared the language of power and authority. As in Zaire it was the creation of a military regime which in Ango-la crushed regional and rural political aspirations. The army gave power and prosperity to its own personnel and sided with the towns against the countryside .... But in Angola the role of the army as cre-ating a trans-ethnic national consciousness was flawed by the fact that the army was used by political authority to maintain control over civilian society during times of austerity and crisis ... it became the agent of control, the defender of wealth in the possessing class, the political elite. ...

Angolan farmers had been harshly integrated into the agrarian mar-ket economy of the last colonial years as cheap labour and as pro-ducers dependent on an exploitative network of rural white traders who had the backing of the state. The collapse of this system, the ending of the opportunities for migrant earnings and the closing down of the rural markets meant that they were wrenched from their limited colonial opportunities and given little or no post-colo-nial alternative means of wealth creation."

Lomelino dos Reis

Lomelino dos Reis is a highly placed officer in the FAA, the govern-ment army, who wants to stay anonymous: "As I served on the front, in the countryside, my eyes were opened about the reasons the war was fought for. This was the first time I was confronted with the poverty of the countryside, people were really starved to death. Many military are really fed up with this war. It serves no one except the people in power. There is enormous corruption going on, also in the military where people are promoted to the rank of Gener-al not because they are the best soldiers to do the job, but because they are loyal to the nepotist state. In this respect, the army suf-fered a lot after abolition of the role of the party inside the army in 1991. A kind of feudal system of dependents of the regime has come in its place.

Combined with the fact that in the state, as well as in the army, there is a real network of *mestiços* protecting each other, this makes things very difficult in the army. One of the other problems is that many of the high government officials thought that they would lose the elections, and so they 'organised' their personal wealth before 1992, thus ruining a big part of the economy. Unfortunately, they won the elections, and now they have to govern a country they ruined themselves and we are confronted with this enormous corruption. If all the money that has been exported out of the country by UNITA, as well as government officials, were returned, we would not have a problem in starting joint ventures with foreigners - the capital would be there to invest! And we need investment to be able to create jobs, if only for the demobilizing military! We could very well start big experimental farms for many ex-soldiers, but the government is not investing in peace, nor is UNITA. Widespread corruption thrives more during war - or this 'no war - no peace' situation than in a real peace.

We need a third political way, apart from the two warring parties. But until now, all efforts in this direction have been blocked; people who tried to develop these ideas have been either bought, blackmailed, or threatened. Some of the leaders of such parties, who worked for the state oil company, have been fired from their jobs!"

Grassroots development: people decide for themselves

Despite the obstacles, and the appearance of a hopeless situation, evidence from the *musseques* indicates that there is a light at the end of the long tunnel. The aim of this book is to look into the lives of people to see how, day after day, they protect themselves, through their own endeavours, from the hazards and pains caused by living in the wreckage of Angola.

We are convinced that, out of these ruins, real development for the Angolan people is only possible by listening carefully to the people who have managed to maintain themselves throughout the war. The methods of 'grassroots' development that have been implemented in Angola so far, for instance by Development Workshop, show promising results. Such projects work under the premise that

people can decide their own fate: it is them, it is the community itself, that counts. You could also say that, especially in Angola, with long traditions of top-down structures, that the last and only solution for the enormous problems the country is confronted with, is a bottom-up approach to development.

We believe that a bottom-up approach will not be in vain, and that Angolan people are capable of developing their own lives, their own families, their own communities, their own organisations, their own municipalities and their own country. However, they need help in the form of aid, and donors should keep on shouting "stop the war", because without peace people will not have the opportunity to help themselves. No government, however willing they are, can ever take care of their citizens if they are constantly obliged to fight a war.

Angolan people also need help in allowing them the conditions to help themselves. The funds made available from abroad for the Local Initiatives Fund that Rui Ricardo runs, are a good example of this. Help is needed to start the enormous task of undoing the continuing horrors of war. This is a forbidding prospect, considering the fact that Angola has one of the highest numbers of land mines in the world: approximately 10 million are hidden in Angola's soil - one for every citizen.

But Angolans must be allowed to work the problems out themselves, to decide for themselves. This is the only solution, a solution that will take decades, but in the end will prove to be the only viable one.

ADRA

Fernando Pacheco, president of ADRA, one of Angola's leading development NGOs, sees it this way: "ADRA is non-governmental, independent, non-party, non-religious, non-profit making, but above all we see ourselves as a social intervention project with the aim to build mutual respect for diversity, pluralism and build a democratic, participatory democracy. How do we do that? We combine two kinds of projects: first of all, community projects at grassroots level, combining practical development with emergency aid, but before anything else, with training to strengthen communities and help them to organise themselves to make them self-sufficient. We have established quite a few of these projects, in three provinces (Huila, Malanje and Benguela) as well as in Luanda, in the *musseque* district of Hoyi ya Henda.

Secondly, we try to promote the culture of debate and thinking, which in our view is the basis of a real civil society. We organise activities such as seminars, conferences and workshops around important national issues, and we debate on the radio; we call it 'the battle of ideas'.

Thirdly, we try to strengthen other emerging groups or NGOs that have the potential to become civic organisations. We try to form a network of concerned people and organisations, not to fight about problems, but to cooperate and to see how we can solve problems together.

Angola is a wrecked country, with the war as the main destructor of (human) capital. Economically, we may be able to repair this wreckage in a couple of decades, but the social disruption will take even longer."

Strategic objectives for civil society

Apart from a peacekeeping, or maybe even peacemaking role for the United Nations, today and in the future, what can the international community do for Angola?

As David Birmingham said: "Demilitarisation is not the only key to success. The political process also requires that each and every section of the society feels that its interests have been fairly presented, heard and incorporated into a truly national agenda. ...

Losers cannot be allowed to feel too harshly betrayed. The demilitarisation of politics, the reconciliation of the ethnic segments ...,
the continued broadening of the democratic process will lower the
temperature of confrontation ...."
True and wise words of an historian, but can they be implemented
in a ruined country? All analysts, historians, politicians and 'devel-
opers', at home and abroad, agree that it will take decades for true
reconciliation and the development of a participatory democracy.
If the international community tries to repeat its efforts of 1992,
to solve the problems with a single round of elections, it will fail
again.
What is necessary is an open eye for 'grassroots development', a
model in which the people concerned matter most, and in which
people decide about their own future, their own development. As
we have seen in this book, Angolans have had to look after themselves for many years, and this experience is of great advantage for
a participatory approach to development, closely linked to

democratisation, economic as well as political, of the country. From this perspective ADRA has formulated three strategic objectives:

1 To work with local communities based on their needs and their aims, taking into account their ethnic and cultural diversity and the plurality of ways of life, in preparing and promoting participatory projects to help development;

2 To support research into alternative development, based on the Angolan reality, and to use practice, particularly in grassroots projects, to develop appropriate methods of work;

3 To contribute towards the strengthening of civil society and the democratisation process taking place in Angola.

Even before the formulation of these objectives, the Sambizanga Project of Development Workshop, where Rui and Zeca Ricardo work, began to develop slowly but surely. The pilot phase of this project has been successfully completed and now the project deserves every support to ensure more projects to give people the opportunity to help themselves in building up their own area, their own organisations, their own lives.

But apart from this kind of urban upgrading project, ADRA proposes other ways in which the development of Angolan society deserves support:

"At a national level, ADRA is now a structured organisation with a certain executive capacity and enjoying considerable credibility. But it is in no way ADRA's intention to become a powerful organisation acting within a fragile and dependent institutional framework. On the contrary, as part of its second strategic objective to strengthen civil society ADRA tries to support the emergence and consolidation of other NGOs, community based organisations and associations, which are organising individuals and groups in similar ways and with similar objectives. ADRA's final aim is to contribute to a setting up of a network of organisations and individuals that work in this way." (Fernando Pacheco, *Why Angola Matters*)

It would be wise of foreign NGOs to act and invest in accordance with the principles articulated here by a truly Angolan intellectual voice, and thereby help emerging Angolan NGOs with institutional support to develop themselves in order to help their members to develop. Not only in this respect are there plenty of opportunities for investment by international donors; investment in civil society has many more aspects, the media, for instance. In colonial times the media were subordinate to Portuguese censorship, in the socialist era they were subordinate to the party's goals. The result is that today there is no independent non-government, non-MPLA, radio station or newspaper. In addition, support for Angolan associations so that they can organise themselves, as well as support for an independent media, can contribute a great deal to the strengthening of civil society. Some changes in legislation have been made, but changes in the government's and UNITA's attitudes towards a free press are doubtful, considering the numerous threats to independent journalists, as reported by Human Rights Watch in 1995: "both the government and UNITA are responsible for the intimidation, detention and killing of journalists".

It is not the political opposition that needs priority support for the development of their media. Much more, it is civil society as a whole that should be supported in developing new media. An Angolan development press is necessary to discuss issues among estab-

lished and emerging NGOs, farmers' associations and trade unions need access to community radio stations to improve their work, churches can be encouraged to publish and someone should start a business press.

In this respect, Fernando Pacheco again speaks a true word: "The bipolarisation of Angola is a potential evil that has to be fought against as a very first step in strengthening civil society. After 1990, space has continued to open up for independent and autonomous organisations, like ours. But don't misunderstand us; our position is not that we are antigovernment! We are non-governmental!"

Epilogue

Once more let us turn to the words of some of the leading characters of this book. Fatima, Zeca, Rui and Pai Ricardo, Ambrosio Pimentel, Adão Cumandala and Teresa Correia Gomez told us their dreams for the future. No better epilogue can be imagined.

Ambrosio Pimentel

"My brother and I would like to go back to Piri, to reactivate the coffee plantation, but also to plant bananas and the like. But this is only possible in peacetime. With a little bit of finance we could produce a lot of coffee, the farm is several hundred acres. Even if we produce a few hundred bags we could start exporting and build up the farm, little by little. I wouldn't even mind if UNITA governs the province there, as long as they leave us in peace. We are farmers, we just want to be able to work, we're sure to stick to the law."

Fatima Ricardo

"Once the roads are open again Ambrosio can travel to Piri, as he used to do before the war of 1992. He always provided us with food from his parents' farm. Maybe Ambrosio will even return to build up his farm again, once the war is really over. But I certainly won't go: I have lived here in town since 1978 and I've got used to life here. Life in the countryside is not as free as it is here. Besides, I have learned to make my living here.

Anyway, in Piri there are no schools for the children and I want them to learn more than I did; and Pango, where I come from, is even worse than Piri. And I don't see how I could work as a profession-

al in Piri - even if there is a school for the children: the only possibility for work would be farming, and that's what I'm doing here
already on our fields in Futungo.
If peace ever returns, I would prefer to work again, not to stay at
the market. I would like to take up my profession as a secretary, or
another new profession. But these jobs will only become available
if enterprises start functioning again, maybe after the war."

Zeca Ricardo
"Personally, I would like to stay working for Development Workshop, but I'd rather be a driver. As soon as I can save the money for
a driving licence I will start. Such a course costs US$100. But, if the
end of the war would give me an opportunity, I would really like to
finish my schooling. I did nine years and would like to finish secondary school, even pre-university.
You know, this would be of great importance. Most people here
stop learning after four or five years of primary school. From there

on, school is more expensive and there are fewer schools. Here in our area, there is only one secondary school with more than 2,500 students, and it costs a lot of money. It would be great to have more secondary schools in the area."

Rui Ricardo

"If I have to stop working for the Sambizanga Project, I won't be out of work entirely. I still have my place at the primary school as a teacher. Or maybe I could apply for the work I did in the project in another area of town, maybe even in another province. I would like to pass the experience we have gained here on to other people in other projects.

But also, within the school system I could pass on this kind of experience. I know a lot of school directors, so we could try to go on with projects on our own. Or, I could teach at secondary school.

Anyway, I don't see myself sitting idle. I'm not used to it, I prefer working, not sitting."

Pai Ricardo

"Quite a few members of our family still live in Pango, but we have no information about them. We don't know whether they are dead or alive. We don't even know about the fate of my wife's mother.

For myself, I would go back to Pango if possible, but I hope to do that with at least one of my sons, with Zeca or Rui and their wives. Of course, they don't know anything about farming, but I could teach them. With a bit of money we could hire a workforce, I know how to plant and grow coffee, and even without electricity we could rebuild the house.

I would prefer to go back; life is more normal there, quieter and cheaper. You can grow everything you need there, except clothes, soap and fuel. But for the rest, everything grows there, all the food you need, except rice. There is cassava, maize, beans, bananas, pineapple, potatoes, sweet potatoes, everything. The worst of it all is that it is so near and still beyond our reach. We used to drive there in five or six hours before the war!"

Adão Cumandala

"After I returned from the front, I just wanted to do something other than fighting, but it wasn't easy to find a job. We had no money, so first I had to find work. The country is in ruins, so there simply is no work. I tried to get work through different schemes, and to do courses. I applied with a lot of friends - up to the level of Colonel - for work in the oil sector, cement sector, diamonds, but nothing worked. The only possibility was Roque Santeiro, selling whatever I could, like everyone else. I sold beer, I worked on a *kandongeiro* - everything. Much later, I heard from a friend about the job I have now [Mr. Cumandala manages a building workshop, *Ed.*]. So for me the problem was over, but many of my friends were not that lucky. I would like to try to start studying again, but first I have to establish the minimal conditions for a decent life for my family. Afterwards, I would like to have a good education suitable for civilian life. A military education isn't worth much in that respect!"

Teresa Correia Gomez

"If I could decide for myself, I would really like to go back to Lubango, to do a project similar to what I'm doing here with community groups. I admit that people here in Luanda need my work, but my heart lies in Lubango. Most of my friends live there, and I lived there for eight important years.

People here in town are not well educated. Many of them think they will find schools here, but they forget about education once they get here. Schools may be better here, but the very bad living conditions have a harmful influence on people. And besides, there are too many people living here. Once the war is over, I hope that a lot of people who fled to town will return to their birthplace. Of course they will need help to do so; many of their villages have been destroyed. I really think that one of the big problems here in Luanda is that so many people from different places have migrated into this city. They come from all the provinces, sometimes hundreds of kilometres away. And all these people, from all these different places, with all their different customs arrived in this melting pot. Many of them cannot maintain themselves here, creating enormous problems, and a whole lot of confusion.

Once the people who want to return have done so, Luanda would become a better place to live for those who stay. Many of them want to stay because of the schools for their children. But they would not consider staying if they were sure there would be good schools in the provinces. That's what I would like to contribute to: schools and other facilities in the provinces, so that people can lead a better life there, instead of being forced to stay here."

Appendix A

Some basic indicators of Angola

Area		1,246,700 sq km
Population		9.7 million
Gross Domestic Product per capita		US$221.9

Infant mortality (per 1,000 births)		160
Under five mortality (per 1,000 births)		292
Life expectancy at birth		45 years
Maternal death rate (per 100,000 births)		665
Access to health services		30 %
Population per physician		15,400
Access to safe water		30 % of total population
Births assisted by trained personnel		15.9 %
Contraceptive use		3.3 %

Adult literacy rate:	women	23 %
	men	50 %
Primary school enrolment		44 %

Completion of first four years of schooling:

Luanda	girls	20 %
	boys	35 %

Students reaching secondary school:

	women	1.7 %
	men	3.3 %

Formal sector employment:	women	20 %
	men	80 %

Informal sector employment:	women	55 %
	men	45 %

(Courtesy, Hurlich, Susan *et al.* 1991. *Angola Country Gender Analysis,* data 1985-1990)

Appendix B

Historical overview of Angola

It is clear that events in Luanda cannot be observed independently from Angola's history. Although a complete history is beyond the scope of this book, we thought that a short chronology for those not familiar with the country would be of help.

Angola is "a country of riches" (Walker, 1990), a fact not unnoticed by wealth seekers from around the world. From the end of the fifteenth century, the greedy of Angola and the rest of the world have each tried to command these riches. Unfortunately for the vast majority of Angolan people, that process continues still. So we start with this brief historical overview with the arrival of the first foreign exploiters of Angola:

1483 First Portuguese arrive, contact with the Kongo Kingdom. Soon missionaries arrive and slave and ivory exports start.

1530 Slave export is an important trade: over 300 years four million Angolans were exported to Brazil and Mexico. In total, 12 million are estimated to have died, as only one quarter of slaves arrived alive.

1571 Gold mines were discovered, and the Portuguese kings decide to capture the Kingdom of Angola. Luanda was founded in 1575 by the Portuguese expeditionary force. Ngola Kiluanje and Rainha Zinga are great names of the Angolan resistance, but the Portuguese had the guns.

1641- 1648 Short intermezzo: the Dutch occupy Luanda and Benguela.

1700 Large parts of Angola are occupied by the Portuguese: slaves are abducted from all over the country for export to Brazil, also a Portuguese colony.

1840 Traders and planters invade the country. Beginning of 100 years of Portuguese conquest of the still unoccupied parts of the country. The era of cotton, rubber and coffee plantations begins.

1899 Forced labour is legally permitted, although slavery was officially abolished in 1834. It makes no difference to the Angolan workers.

1902 Until 1920 several uprisings of the Angolans, especially the Bakongo and Umbundu.

1912 First diamond mines established.

1920 Portuguese declare Angola 'pacified': from now on Portuguese civil, instead of military, authorities run the country.

1950 Massive influx of Portuguese settlers. The settler population grows steadily until independence in 1975; by then 350,000 Portuguese live in the country.

1956 The earlier founded independence movement 'Party of the United Struggle of Africans of Angola' (PLUA) becomes the Movimento Popular de Libertação de Angola (MPLA). It is this party that now dominates the government.

1961 Uprising among cotton workers in Malanje. The MPLA tries to liberate prisoners from the Luanda prison. Uprisings all over the country. Generally seen as the year of the beginning of the independence struggle. Three hundred settlers killed, subsequently 20,000 Angolans killed by the Portuguese.

1962 The Union of Populations of North Angola (UPA) merges with other movements to become the FNLA (Frente Nacional de Libertação de Angola) and forms a government in exile in Kinshasa, Zaire. Through President Mobutu it obtains support from the USA, while the MPLA, with headquarters in Brazzaville obtains mainly Soviet Russian aid.

1965 The MPLA intensifies the guerilla war, mainly in the province of Moxico. Portugal strikes back with NATO and US support. Oil (from the enclave of Cabinda) now is the major reason for the colonialist power to stay.

1966 UNITA (União Nacional para a Independencia Total de Angola) under Jonas Savimbi splits from FNLA. It obtains support from China, and later South Africa. It is mainly supported by Ovimbundus.

1974 Angola's three liberation movements do not perform very well, also due to a lack of unity. But in Portugal a dramatic change (the April 'coup of captains') leads to an attempt to unite the three movements and to grant independence to Angola.

1975 It is a crucial year for Angola: in January, the Alvor agreement between FNLA, UNITA and the MPLA is signed, to be broken by February. Zaire and USA (CIA) back FNLA, Cuba supports the MPLA from May onward in the fierce struggles that break out. In July, the MPLA has full control over Luanda. South Africa enters the scene militarily and invades from the south. In October, joint MPLA and Cuban forces stop the South African column just outside Luanda. In November, the last Portuguese troops depart and Agostinho Neto, president of the MPLA, is sworn in as

President of Angola. US Congress stops aid for UNITA and FNLA, and from now on Gulf oil pays for the oil from Cabinda to the new Angolan (MPLA) government.

1976   All invaders are successively thrown out of the country, leaving behind massive destruction throughout, especially in the south.

1977   Dramatic changes inside the MPLA: the 'hawks' win and the communist rule starts. An attempted coup in Luanda ('Nito Alves coup') is put down.

1979   President Neto dies and is succeeded by an oil engineer, José Eduardo dos Santos, still President of the Republic in 1996.

1981   With support of Ronald Reagan, South Africans start invading again. Their support for UNITA has consequences for the population of the whole of Angola.

1984   Cease-fire signed in Lusaka, broken soon.

1986   USA now openly supports UNITA.

1987   Open fighting between South Africans and Cuban troops occurs, ending in the 'battle of Cuito Cuanavale'.

1988   Agreement between South Africa, Angola, Cuba and the USA, resulting in withdrawal of the Cubans and independence of Namibia (effective in 1990).

1989   Peace talks in Gbadolite, Zaire; cease-fire collapses almost immediately.

1990   Accord of Bicesse, leading to a Peace Agreement in May 1991 between the MPLA and UNITA. Angola is no longer a socialist state. Free trade, free movement, free speech and free elections are guaranteed.

1992   After difficult but internationally declared free and fair elections, UNITA withdraws its troops from the (not yet fully formed) united national army, declares the elections a fraud because Savimbi lost the Presidency and starts to fight again, now from much more advantageous military positions than ever. Fierce fighting in November in Luanda, but UNITA is thrown out of town again. Fighting in all other provinces continues and makes Luanda one of the few safe places in the country.

1994   Again peace talks in Portugal, Addis Abeba and finally in Lusaka where the last peace agreement was signed, but until 1996 not implemented in the whole of Angola, to great disappointment of the majority of the Angolan people.

Adapted from: Sogge, David, *et al.* 1992. *Sustainable Peace, Angola's recovery.* SARDC, Harare; with additional information by the editor.

Glossary of Angolan-Portuguese words, organisations and abbreviations

ADRA	Associação de Desenvolvimento Rural e Ambiente - one of Angola's main development NGOs
Amigos do meio Ambiente	Friends of the Environment, youth association in Ngola Kiluanje
bombom	cassava root (Kimbundu)
Cacuaco	village on the sea, just outside Ngola Kiluanje
campo	countryside
compra e venda	buy and sell - also used for making a living in the informal economy
confusão	confusion, generally used for quarrel, row, riot, revolt, even the war raging in Luanda between October 31 and November 2, 1992
deslocados	displaced persons - refugees inside Angola
Development Workshop	Canadian/Angolan NGO mainly working on urban upgrading projects in the *musseques* of Luanda, funded by Canadian and European donors
DNA	National water authority of Angola
EDEL	Municipal electricity authority, Luanda
ELISAL	Municipal rubbish removal authority, Luanda
EPAL	Municipal water authority, Luanda
FAA	(Unified) Angolan Army: unified before 1992, afterwards without UNITA, now the government's army
fazenda	farm
FNLA	Frente Nacional de Libertação de Angola, originally a freedom movement, later in armed opposition against the MPLA, now in opposition in the parliament
fuba	cassava meal (Kimbundu)
funje	cassava porridge
Futungo	Municipality in the south of Luanda - the presidential palace is situated here
FONGA	Organisation of Angolan NGOs
gazosa	soft drink, also used to mean a tip or bribe (f.i. of police)

guia de marcha	travel permit, necessary for Angolan citizens travelling outside their own province
kandonga	'free' market: prohibited until 1990, since then the commercial standard
kandongeiro	roving collective taxi, also a 'free' salesman
Kaxito	provincial capital of the province of Bengo, just north of Luanda
Kimbundu	African Language spoken around Luanda
kizaka	a vegetable dish of cassava leaves
Kota	Uncle (Kimbundu)
Kwanza	name of the river south of Luanda, name of the provinces around Luanda, name of the Angolan currency, name of a big market in Ngola Kiluanje
Mae	Mum, Mother
mestiços	people of mixed Portuguese and African race
musseque	shantytowns outside the city, originally townships; from 'mu seke', meaning 'area of the sand'
NGO	Nongovernmental (development) organisation, only permitted in Angola since 1991.
Ngola Kiluanje who	commune named after the Angolan King of Ndongo, fought the Portuguese until his death in 1617
Ovimbundu	African language spoken around the central highlands of Huambo
Pai	Dad, Father
praça (praçita)	small square, also used for (small) market
Piri	village in the province of Kwanza Norte
Programma de aterro de lixo	rubbish dump removal project
Rainha Zinga	daughter of Ngola Kiluanje, lived from 1581-1663, fought the Portuguese for over 30 years
Roque Santeiro	big *kandonga* on the former rubbish dump and public execution place of Luanda
Sambizanga	old *musseque* municipality, famous for its revolutionary behaviour against the Portuguese
Secafe	state secretariat for coffee
Soba	traditional headman

Bibliography

A. Further reading

Angola Peace Monitor. Produced every month by ACTSA - Action for Southern Africa. ACTSA, 28 Penton Street, London N1 9SA; email actsa@geo2.poptel.org.uk; fax 44 171 837 3001, telephone 44 171 833 3133. One year's subscription: UK£10 in the U.K.

Hart, Keith and Joanna Lewis. 1995. *Why Angola Matters.* African Studies Centre, University of Cambridge with James Currey, London.

Minter, William. 1994. *Apartheid's Contras,* Zed Books, London/New Jersey.

One World Action. 1994. *Angola, Building for the future, despite the world's worst war*, One World Action, London.

Sogge, David, *et al.* 1992. *Sustainable Peace, Angola's recovery.* SARDC, Harare.

Vieira, Jose Luandino. 1980. *Luuanda.* African Writers Series, Heinemann, London.

Walker, Graham. 1990. Angola: *The Promise of Riches.* Zed Press, London.

Woolfers, Michael and Bergerol, Jane. 1983. *Angola in the front line.* Zed Press, London.

Roskam, Karel. 1992. *Development and democracy in Angola.* African European Institute, Amsterdam.

B. Sources of inspiration for this book

Bender, Gerald 1991. *The Luanda Household Budget and Nutrition Survey.* Food Studies Group, University of Oxford, Oxford.

Care International. no date. *Angola Small Enterprise Sector Assessment.* Care International, Angola.

Comercio Actualidade. 1995-96. Luanda.

Daly, Mary. 1991. *Urbanisation of Luanda and Local Government.* Development Workshop, Luanda.

Development Workshop. 1995. *Abastecimento de Agua e Saneamento, seus Problemas Urbanos: Avaliação dos Benificiarios para Luanda.* Development Workshop, Luanda.

Development Workshop. 1995. *Women's Enterprise Development in Luanda.* Development Workshop, Luanda.

Humbi Humbi Quarterly. 1994-96. ADRA-Angola, Luanda.

Hurlich, Susan *et al.* 1991. *Angola Country Gender Analysis.* DW, Luanda.

Lewis, Oscar. 1961. *Five Families*, Penguin Modern Classics. Harmondsworth, England.

Luanda Development Planning. 1995. *Projectos Urbanisticos Integrados.* Briefing from Luanda Development Planning, Luanda.

Ntyamba, Jorge. 1994. *Huambo, 56 Dias de Terror e Morte*, Jango, Luanda.

Posthumus, Bram. 1996. 'Profiteers cause stagnation' in *Internationale Samenwerking*, March.

Robson, Paul. 1992. *Musseque Neighbourhood Upgrading Project.* One World Action, London.

da Silva, João Francisco. 1995. *Luanda - crescimento da cidade*, working paper, Luanda.

Vieira, Jose Luandino. 1980. *A Vida Secreta de Domingos Xavier.* Jango, Luanda.

Colophon

A family of the musseque was first published by
WorldView Publishing, 1996

Copyright © Bob van der Winden, 1996

Design by Jan Vos, Medio, Amsterdam
Set in Lucida by Medio, Amsterdam
Printed by Raddraaier, Amsterdam, The Netherlands
English editing: Geraldine Reardon

Text and pictures by: Alexia Gamito, João Francisco da Silva,
Pascoal Estevão, Jack Ramiro, Vicente Albino Paulo (Genuíno),
Victor Vunge and Bob van der Winden

Editor: Bob van der Winden

A British Library Cataloguing in Publication record is available for this book

ISBN: 1 872142 32 x   hardback
ISBN: 1 872142 33 8   paperback

Published by   WorldView Publishing, P.O. Box 595, Oxford OX26YH, UK
Tel. +44 (0) 185 201562, Fax +44 (0) 1865 201906
email: worldview@patrol.i-way.co.uk

Distributed in the Netherlands by:
De Verbeelding Ltd, 40 Utrechtsestraat, 1017 VP Amsterdam, The Netherlands;
Tel: 31 20 626 5385, Fax: 31 20 625 7209

Distributed in the U.S.A.by:
Africa Policy Information Center,
110 Maryland Ave. NE, #509, Washington, DC 20002.
Tel: 1 202 546 7961; Fax: 1 202 546 1545; E-mail: apic@igc.apc.org.

Also distributed by:
Development Workshop, Angola, Canada, France
Holland Committee on Southern Africa, The Netherlands

Partly financed by the European Commission DG VIII